changing the way the world learns

To get extra value from this book for no additional cost, go to:

http://www.thomson.com/wadsworth.html

thomson.com is the World Wide Web site for Wadsworth/ITP and is your direct source to dozens of on-line resources. *thomson.com* helps you find out about supplements, experiment with demonstration software, search for a job, and send e-mail to many of our authors. You can even preview new publications and exciting new technologies.

thomson.com: *It's where you'll find us in the future.*

Crime and the American Dream

Second Edition

STEVEN F. MESSNER
University at Albany, S. U. N. Y.

RICHARD ROSENFELD
University of Missouri—St. Louis

WITHDRAWN

Wadsworth Publishing Company
I⟨T⟩P® An International Thomson Publishing Company

Belmont, CA • Albany, NY • Bonn • Boston • Cincinnati • Detroit • Johannesburg
London • Madrid • Melbourne • Mexico City • New York • Paris
Singapore • Tokyo • Toronto • Washington

Sociology Editor: Eve Howard
Assistant Editor: Deirdre McGill
Marketing Manager: Chaun Hightower
Senior Project Editor: Debby Kramer
Production: Merrill Peterson/Matrix Productions
Print Buyer: Karen Hunt
Permissions Editor: Jeanne Bosschart
Copy Editor: Laura Larson
Cover Designer: Laurie Anderson
Compositor: Thompson Type
Printer: Edwards Brothers/Ann Arbor

For additional credits, see page xvi.

Printed in the United States of America
2 3 4 5 6 7 8 9 10

For more information, contact Wadsworth Publishing Company, 10 Davis Drive, Belmont, California
94002 USA

International Thomson Publishing Europe
Berkshire House 168-173
High Holborn
London, WC1V 7AA
England

Thomas Nelson Australia
102 Dodds Street
South Melbourne 3205
Victoria, Australia

Nelson Canada
1120 Birchmount Road
Scarborough, Ontario
Canada M1K 5G4

International Thomson Publishing GmbH
Königswinterer Strasse 418
53227 Bonn, Germany

International Thomson Editores
Campos Eliseos 385, Piso 7
Col. Polanco
11560 México D.F. México

International Thomson Publishing Asia
221 Henderson Road
#05-10 Henderson Building
Singapore 0315

International Thomson Publishing Japan
Hirakawacho Kyowa Building, 3F
2-2-1 Hirakawacho
Chiyoda-ku, Tokyo 102, Japan

International Thomson Publishing
Southern Africa
Building 18, Constantia Park
240 Old Pretoria Road
Halfway House, 1685 South Africa

Library of Congress Cataloging-in-Publication Data

Messner, Steven F.
    Crime and the American dream / Steven F. Messner, Richard Rosenfeld.—2nd ed.
        p.   cm.—(Contemporary issues in crime and justice series)
    Includes bibliographical references and index.
    ISBN 0-534-51766-8
    1. Criminology—United States.   2. Crime—Sociological aspects—United States.   3. Social
structure—United States.   4. Anomie.
I. Rosenfeld, Richard.   II. Title.   III. Series.
HV6022.U6M47   1997   96-34643
364.973—dc20

Nothing happens unless first a dream.
—Carl Sandburg

Contents

Preface

This book has been written with two purposes in mind. The first is to present a plausible explanation of the exceptionally high levels of serious crime in the United States. The second is to formulate this explanation using the basic ideas, insights, and conceptual tools of sociology.

Each of these purposes rests on an underlying premise, one empirical, the other epistemological. The empirical premise is that crime rates are, in fact, exceptionally high in the United States. Some level of criminal activity may be a normal feature of all societies, as Émile Durkheim proposed almost a century ago. However, both the level of and the preoccupation with serious crime in America are quite striking, especially when the United States is compared with other highly developed nations. Both quantitative and qualitative evidence are reported in the book to support our empirical claim about the distinctiveness of the American experience with crime.

An important epistemological premise also informs our inquiry. We are convinced that the formulation of a satisfactory explanation of cross-national variation in crime will require the systematic application of sociological knowledge and principles, which together comprise the "sociological perspective." Some sociologists will undoubtedly reject the notion that there is any common intellectual terrain that can be so described. Nonetheless, although we recognize the diversity of theoretical and metatheoretical orientations in the field, we are convinced that a set of common concepts and assumptions forms the corpus of the discipline. This is, after all, what we teach our students year after year, and what we require as part of a core curriculum for both graduate and undergraduate students. In a sense, then, we set out in this book to "put sociology to work" on a substantive problem of considerable theoretical and practical significance. The great advantage of the sociological perspective, in our view, is that it requires that attention be paid to both of the fundamental features of any organized social system: people's beliefs, values, goals—the stuff of culture—and the positions and roles that people occupy in society—what sociologists term "social structure." Neither of these two basic features of social organization may be ignored a priori in sociological analysis. It may, of course, turn out that a particular social phenomenon, such as crime, is more heavily dependent on one or the other of these features. But this must be demonstrated; it cannot be assumed. The sociological burden of proof always rests with those who would cast out one of the basic aspects of social organization and privilege the other. The focus on both culture and social structure, and on the interplay between them, has been an invaluable analytical tool for evaluating the strengths and weaknesses of influential explanations of crime, as well as for developing our own thesis.

The essence of our argument is that the distinctive patterns and levels of crime in the United States are produced by the cultural and structural organization of American society. American culture is characterized by a strong emphasis on the goal of monetary success and a weak emphasis on the importance of the legitimate means for the pursuit of success. This combination of strong pressures to succeed monetarily and weak restraints on the selection of means is intrinsic to the dominant cultural ethos: the American Dream. The American Dream contributes to crime directly by encouraging people to employ illegal means to achieve goals that are culturally approved. It also exerts an indirect effect on crime through its interconnections with the institutional balance of power in society.

The American Dream promotes and sustains an institutional structure in which one institution—the economy—assumes dominance over all others. The resulting imbalance in the institutional structure diminishes the capacity of other institutions, such as the family, education, and the political system, to curb criminogenic cultural pressures and to impose controls over the behavior of members of society. In these ways, the distinctive cultural commitments of the American Dream and its companion institutional arrangements contribute to high levels of crime.

Although we began writing this book convinced of the general thesis that high levels of crime in the United States are related to basic features of social organization, we never anticipated many of the specific arguments that have emerged as a result of our intellectual efforts. Novelists and playwrights describe how characters and plot can assume "a life of their own" and lead the author in unforeseen directions. Something like this occurred as we worked our way through the connections between crime and the American Dream. The use of the sociological perspective necessitated a more systematic and critical appraisal of existing theory and research on crime—including our own—than we intended.

At the beginning, we conceived of this book as a summary statement of criminological research within the anomie tradition, where much of our research has been located, and as a call for continued work in this area. However, the sociological perspective led us to rethink some of the basic assumptions and interpretations of anomie theory, such as the presumed association between crime and social stratification. We continue to believe that anomie theory offers significant insights regarding the nature of crime and of the American crime problem in particular. But the contributions of anomie theory, and those of alternative theoretical approaches, will be realized fully only when situated in a more general sociological perspective on crime and social organization.

Writing this book was a process of discovery or, more precisely, rediscovery of the value of the sociological way of viewing the world. Although we have developed an explanation of crime that differs from other explanations in important respects, many of the ideas underlying our explanation are not original; they are part of the common heritage of modern sociology. Our thinking about culture, social structure, and crime fits within an intellectual environment shaped by Émile Durkheim, Alexis de Tocqueville, and Karl Marx. Our analysis of social institutions is highly compatible with the recent contribution of Robert Bellah and his colleagues in *The Good Society*. Our conception of sociological inquiry has been influenced by scholars as diverse as Talcott Parsons and C. Wright Mills, both of whom insisted that the separate parts of a society always must be understood with reference to the whole. Finally, we owe an incalculable intellectual debt to Robert K. Merton, on whose shoulders our sociological explanation of crime stands most directly.

THE PLAN OF THE BOOK

Chapter 1 introduces the central premise of our explanation of crime, namely, that high levels of serious crime result from the normal functioning of the American social system. This chapter also presents the core components of the American Dream. We describe how they contribute to the openness and dynamic quality of American society, as well as to "the dark side" of the American experience: high rates of crime. Chapter 1 ends with a description of Merton's formulation of the anomie perspective on crime. We suggest that, despite ups and downs over time in the appeal of Merton's argument to criminologists, and significant substantive limitations that are addressed in subsequent chapters, anomie theory has enduring value in the study of crime.

In Chapter 2 we describe in detail the nature of the crime problem in the contemporary United States. We present evidence on both "crimes in the streets" and "crimes in the suites" to substantiate the underlying empirical premise of the book, that there is indeed something distinctive about crime and the response to crime in the United States. The descriptive material in Chapter 2 essentially reveals, in the form of statistical indicators and human responses, a social reality of crime that a comprehensive sociological theory must be capable of explaining.

We turn in Chapter 3 to a review of the dominant sociological perspectives in contemporary criminology. We consider the more individualistic, social psychological approaches to crime as well as their macrolevel analogues. Each of the perspectives reviewed contains valuable insights about the origins of crime, but each is also limited in important respects. We propose that, among conventional approaches, the anomie perspective holds the greatest promise for a macrolevel explanation of crime because of its sociological completeness. In contrast with alternative perspectives, anomie theory incorporates into its explanatory framework both cultural and structural dynamics. We also identify the more important limitations of conventional anomie theory, especially the curious neglect of institutional dynamics by supporters and critics alike.

Chapter 4 presents our macrosociological explanation of crime. We identify the anomic tendencies of the American Dream and show how these tendencies are both reflected in and reproduced by an institutional structure dominated by the economy. Our analysis focuses on four major social institutions: the family, the educational system, the political system, and, of course, the economy. We substantiate our claim of institutional imbalance by pointing to three manifestations of economic dominance: (1) the devaluation of noneconomic functions and roles, (2) the accommodation to economic demands required of other institutions, and (3) the penetration into other institutional domains of economic standards. Finally, we discuss the interconnections between anomic cultural orientations, weak institutional control, and levels and patterns of crime.

We conclude in Chapter 5 with an extended discussion of the theoretical and policy implications of the analysis. Our thesis offers a serious challenge to both criminological theorists and policy makers. It implies that criminological theories that neglect the ironic interdependence between crime and the normal functioning of the social system will be unable to explain the American experience with crime. Moreover, if our analysis is valid, significant reductions in crime will not result from conservative "get tough" policies of crime control, nor from conventional liberal proposals to broaden access to the American Dream. Effective crime control will, instead, require fundamental transformations in the organization of American society and a rethinking of a dream that is the envy of the world.

THE REVISED EDITION

The fact that you are reading the preface to the second edition of *Crime and the American Dream* indicates that the first edition attracted sufficient attention to justify the cost to the publisher of producing a new one. In revising the book, we have updated statistical data and introduced new illustrations. We have also made a few substantive revisions that are intended to clarify and strengthen our major arguments, although the core thesis has not been altered in any significant way. We have expanded the discussion in Chapter 2 of cross-national differences in crime to encompass variation in the form as well as the level of offending. In Chapter 3 we have sought to clarify the distinction between "macro" and "micro" levels of analysis with an example that should have particular relevance to college students: the relationship between education and unemployment. In Chapter 4 we extend our basic argument about cross-national differences in crime to account for the social distribution of crime within the United States. This discussion focuses on two of the most important correlates of criminal behavior: gender and race. Finally, throughout the second edition we have incorporated citations to recent scholarship on American culture and institutional structure. Of particular note are Barry Schwartz's insights concerning "economic imperialism" in American society, Jennifer Hochschild's analysis of the American Dream and the racial crisis, and Carl Husemoller Nightingale's juxtaposition of inner-city children's aspirations and life chances.[1]

Above all else, authors want their work to be taken seriously, and we have had the good fortune of receiving serious critical commentary from scholars, students, and other readers. *Crime and the American Dream* was featured in an "Authors-Meet-Critics" session held at the 1994 meeting of the American Society of Criminology. In the course of this intellectual exchange with some of the very best scholars working in criminology today, we received valuable advice regarding the research implications of our analysis. That advice, put most directly by Francis T. Cullen, was in essence "use it or lose it." By this he meant that our ideas about crime must be continuously reexamined and refined in research, for it is in the research process that ideas are "used" by social scientists.

We have begun to confront Cullen's challenge. Since the publication of the first edition, we have sought to elaborate and test some of the implications of our argument, and other researchers have as well.[2] Some of the results of these efforts are reported in Chapter 5. We encourage readers of the new edition to perform their own tests of our ideas against evidence available from other studies and from their personal observations and experiences. In this way, our contribution will not be "lost" even if readers conclude that our account of crime requires more than the modest changes introduced in the new edition.

NOTES

1. Schwartz (1994b); Hochschild (1995); Nightingale (1993).

2. See Messner and Rosenfeld (1994, 1996) and Rosenfeld and Messner (1995, 1996). Chamlin and Cochran (1995) tested hypotheses derived from our argument using data for U.S. states. For a debate over the results of their study, see Jensen (1996) and Chamlin and Cochran (1996).

Acknowledgments

We are grateful to those colleagues who have taken the time to write to us about their own and their students' reactions to *Crime and the American Dream*, and to the reviewers who provided such competent criticism of the first edition and such clear guidance for improving the second. Among the reviewers who offered insightful comments and suggestions on the manuscript were Robert Agnew, Amory University; Thomas J. Bernard, Pennsylvania State University; David Bordua, University of Illinois; Robert J. Bursik, Jr., University of Oklahoma; Mitchell B. Chamlin, University of Cincinnati; Roland Chilton, University of Massachusetts at Amherst; Richard Hawkins, Southern Methodist University; Robert F. Meier, Iowa State University; John Stratton, University of Iowa; and Austin Turk, University of California, Riverside. We made revisions in response to some of those suggestions and sharpened the focus of our arguments in response to others. Serina Beauparlant, our editor at Wadsworth for the first edition, enthusiastically supported the book from the outset. Her enthusiasm bolstered our confidence on more than one occasion when we began to doubt the merits of the project. We also wish to acknowledge the encouragement and patience of Eve Howard, our editor during the preparation of the revised edition. The graphics appearing in Chapters 2, 3, and 4 reflect the skill, patience, and persistence of Richard Rabe and Chris Reichard. Eric Baumer devoted exceptional care and good humor to the task of checking citations and references. Finally, Richard Rosenfeld would like to thank the University of Missouri–St. Louis for a research leave that made it possible to devote sustained attention to the manuscript.

This book is dedicated to our parents, spouses, and children, who have facilitated and tempered our pursuit of the American Dream.

Credits

"The Killing Fields," by Rick Soll is from *Chicago Magazine,* March, 1993, pp. 54–59, 97–99. Reprinted by permission of the publisher.

"Englewood Longs for the Safe Old Days," by Monica Copeland, William Rectenwald, and Sharman Stein is from *The Chicago Tribune,* December 29, 1991, Section 2, pp. 1–3. Adapted by permission of the publisher.

"L.A. Jurors Blinded by Fear of Crime," by Stephen Chapman is from *The St. Louis Post-Dispatch,* May 4, 1992, p. 3B. Stephen Chapman is a writer for *The Chicago Tribune* and syndicated by Creators Syndicate. Used by permission of Creators Syndicate.

Figure 4.1 and excerpts from *The Work and Family Revolution.* Copyright © 1991 by Barbara Vanderkolk and Ardis Armstrong Young. Reprinted with permission by Facts on File, New York, Inc.

"Somalia? In the South Bronx, They Ask, Why Not Aid Us?" by Lynda Richardson, *The New York Times,* December 14, 1992, p. A8. © 1992 The New York Times Company. Reprinted by permission.

"Where Even a Grade School Is No Refuge From Gunfire," by Don Terry, *The New York Times,* October 17, 1992, pp. 1, 6. © 1992 The New York Times Company. Reprinted by permission.

"Korean Shop Owners Fearful of Outcome of Beating Trial," by Seth Mydans, *The New York Times,* April 10, 1993, pp. 1, 12. © 1993 The New York Times Company. Reprinted by permission.

"After Gunman's Acquittal, Japan Struggles to Understand America," by David E. Sanger, *The New York Times,* May 15, 1993, pp. A1, A7. © 1993 The New York Times Company. Reprinted by permission.

"The Body Count at Home," by Jonathan Alter, *Newsweek,* December 28, 1992, p. 55. © 1992 Newsweek, Inc. All rights reserved. Reprinted by permission.

"The Scope and Purposes of Corrections: Exploring Alternative Responses to Crowding," by Richard Rosenfeld and K. Kempf, from *Crime and Delinquency,* Vol. 37, pp. 481–505. Adapted by permission of Sage Publications, Inc.

"Lithuania Is a Snap for U.S.," August 7, 1992, p. D1. Reprinted with permission of the *St. Louis Post-Dispatch,* © 1992.

"Amid Reality of Nightly Gunfights, Residents Stay Committed to Area," by Peter Hernon, October 4, 1992, pp. 1A, 9A. Reprinted with permission of the *St. Louis Post-Dispatch,* © 1992.

"Neighborhood Crime Takes Deadly Toll: Elderly Man Dies After Robbery," by Bill Bryan, August 25, 1992, p. 3A. Reprinted with permission of the *St. Louis Post-Dispatch,* © 1992.

"Student, 17, Fatally Shot at Sumner," by Bill Bryan and Joan Little, March 26, 1993, pp. 1A, 10A. Reprinted with permission of the *St. Louis Post-Dispatch,* © 1993.

"Robert Merton's Contributions to the Sociology of Deviance," by Richard Rosenfeld, 1989, Sociological Inquiry, Vol. 59, pp. 453–466. Reprinted by permission of the publisher.

1

A Society Organized for Crime

Winning isn't everything; it's the only thing.

VINCE LOMBARDI,
FOOTBALL COACH

By any means necessary.

MALCOLM X,
BLACK NATIONALIST

In November 1990, Michael Milken, who headed the high-yield bond department of Drexel Burnham Lambert, was sentenced to ten years in prison for violating federal securities laws. The indictment against Milken charged that he had earned as much as $550 million in a single year from his illegal activities; at sentencing, the loss from Milken's violations was estimated at a much lower but still considerable figure of approximately $318,000.[1] A *New York Times* editorial supported the stiff penalty handed down by federal Judge Kimba Wood, which also included a three-year term of probation, 5,400 hours of community service, and over $1 billion in fines and restitution. The *Times* observed that Judge Wood had sent a "wake-up call" to the financial community that the days of "wrist-slapping" for crimes committed on Wall Street were over.[2]

Milken had pioneered the use of high-risk, high-yield bonds as instruments to facilitate swift corporate buyouts and takeovers. Although critics viewed the so-called "junk bond" as a destructive weapon of corporate warfare, Milken saw his financial innovations as part of a mission to reform the American economy. Even the *New York Times* appeared to agree with at least some aspects of Milken's positive self-assessment. Just five days after advocating strong punishments to send messages to Wall Street, the *Times* published another editorial warning against "premature moralizing" about Milken's role in a "decade of greed." He had, after all, used the junk bond to provide much needed credit for hundreds of new companies. For those able to survive the recession, the *Times* suggested, Milken's innovative legacy would look brighter.

1

Judge Kimba Wood evidently shared the *Times's* ambivalence about Milken's misdeeds, for she reduced his prison sentence from ten years to two years in August 1992 in return for his cooperation in a subsequent investigation.[3]

Since his release from prison, Milken has applied his considerable energy to counseling corporate leaders who regard him as a "financial visionary," promoting research to find a cure for prostate cancer, and teaching courses at UCLA's graduate business school. The idea of a convicted white-collar criminal teaching business students has elicited contradictory reactions. For example, a UCLA science student remarked, "I resent Milken's being here.... This is an institution of higher education, not a place for opportunists to make money." In contrast, another student described Milken as "a great man—a martyr, not a crook." Both students seem to be responding to many of the same qualities in Milken, especially what one journalist has called his "bottom-line fanaticism" and innovative spirit.[4]

In a final note of irony to the Milken story, Judge Wood has been characterized in legal circles in terms strikingly similar to those applied to Michael Milken, as an independent and intelligent judge willing to pursue "innovative solutions" to legal problems. Several of Judge Wood's legal opinions are considered "creative and unusual," according to a *New York Times* report on her nomination in 1993 for attorney general by President Bill Clinton. Judge Wood subsequently withdrew her nomination after reports that, like the president's previous nominee Zoe Baird, she had employed an illegal alien to care for her children.[5]

The Michael Milken story illustrates the paradoxes inherent in the sources of and responses to crime in the United States. The very qualities in which Milken took pride and for which he was praised—his daring, energy, intelligence, and, most important, his ability to create and willingness to use innovative solutions for conventional problems—also led to his crimes and punishment. These qualities are not merely the personal traits of a particular criminal (or "economic reformer"); they are elements of social character rooted in broad value orientations within American culture that help shape both the archetypal American hero and the archetypal American villain. An even more fundamental sociological principle is revealed by the Milken case: the ironic interdependence between good and evil in social life. As the sociologist Kai Erikson explains, "the deviant and the conformist . . . are creatures of the same culture, inventions of the same imagination."[6] To understand fully the nature and level of crime in a society, therefore, it is essential to consider the distinguishing features of that society, particularly its distinctive cultural imagination.

CRIME AND RESPONSES
TO CRIME IN AMERICA

The ironic interdependence of deviance and conformity applies not only to the kinds of financial crimes for which Milken was convicted but to crime more generally, including crimes of violence. Indeed, although property crimes and violent crimes might appear on the surface to be quite different, many violent crimes are similar to the so-called "suite" crimes of high finance in an important respect: they involve a willingness to innovate, that is, to use technically efficient but illegitimate means to solve conventional problems.

The Nature and Level of Criminal Violence

Fictional accounts of violent crime frequently involve exotic motives and elaborate planning. In fact, much criminal violence is quite mundane. It is the outcome of a commonplace dispute between a victim and an offender who know one another. These disputes often arise from economic transactions gone awry. The following scenarios, drawn from police case files in St. Louis, illustrate the role of homicide in settling disputes related to drug transactions:[7]

> Suspect bought two bags of coke from victim. One of the bags was not dope. Suspect followed victim and witness in a car. Victim stopped his car, got out, and began approaching suspect's car. Suspect opened fire. Victim dead on scene.

> Victim was a "runner"—delivering drugs for a seller. He was nervous because he was short his "turn in." A friend lent him $2,500 cash the evening before the victim was killed. Victim liked to "flash" cash and expensive jewelry, and talk about what he could afford to buy. The seller denied having anything to do with victim's death. He was later murdered.

> Police were looking for seller so he gave victim his stash to hold for him. Victim refused to return it. On night of shooting, victim had gone to White Castle with her husband. While he was out of the car, victim disappeared, apparently abducted by suspects. According to a secret witness, victim was shot while sitting in the car with two suspects at location where car was found. Victim had ripped off dealers several times by never paying in full or driving off with drugs. Victim had once been ripped off herself when dealer took her money and did not give her drugs.

A common theme running through these events is an economic dispute that is settled by the use of violent means. The disputes arise from economic problems that are quite conventional in origin (faulty or fraudulent merchandise, payments overdue, bad debts, common thefts). However, none of these problems or the resulting disputes can be settled through conventional (that is, legal) means, because they all involve illegal activities. Because access to conventional dispute resolution mechanisms (lawyers, courts, legally imposed restitution, fines, and so forth) is blocked in these cases, their resolution requires the innovative use of unconventional means. Many crimes, including homicides, have been characterized as a form of "self-help" directed at rule infractions for which conventional legal responses are either ineffective or, as in these cases, unavailable.[8]

The use of violent means to achieve or regain control in underworld markets, like the use of illegal nonviolent means (such as price fixing or insider trading) to control legitimate markets, receives strong, if indirect, cultural support in our society. High rates of gun-related violence, in particular, result in part from a cultural ethos that encourages the rapid deployment of technically efficient methods to solve interpersonal problems. The widespread availability of firearms, and their use by offenders and rule enforcers alike, represent not simply the strength or persistence of a "gun culture," which itself requires explanation, but a much deeper cultural orientation that permits or does not strongly discourage the attainment of goals "by any means necessary."

This "anything goes" mentality results in a volume of criminal violence in the United States that is truly remarkable. Consider levels of the most serious violent crime: homicide. More than 23,000 homicides were reported to the police the year that Michael Milken went to prison. The U.S. homicide rate is higher than that of nearly all other developed nations in the world.[9] In 1992, more homicides occurred in St. Louis (population 390,000) than in the entire nation of Scotland (population 5,100,000)—and Scottish homicide levels are considered high by European standards.[10]

Fear of Crime

Not surprisingly, high levels of violent crime in the United States result in widespread fear of crime. Forty-seven percent of the adult population—and over half of black American adults—are afraid to walk alone at night in their own neighborhoods.[11] In the inner cities, parents sometimes feel compelled to keep their children inside—a confinement that young people refer to as "lockdown," an ironic term borrowed from the lexicon of prison life.[12] Fear of crime has been shown to reduce residents' satisfaction with their neighborhood and to instill a desire to abandon the neighborhood for safer surroundings. One observer has suggested that fear of crime, more than racial prejudice, explains why a California jury found four white police officers not guilty in the widely publicized beating in Los Angeles of Rodney King, a black man, that sparked protests and rioting in the spring of 1992.[13]

The pervasive fear of crime observed in the United States is not an inevitable feature of modern, industrial societies. On the contrary, it is a distinctly American phenomenon. Freda Adler, a comparative criminologist who has studied crime in many nations throughout the modern world, concludes that the American

> preoccupation with crime is not a national past-time in more countries than one. Neither the design of doors and windows, nor the front page stories in the national press, nor the budgetary allocations of municipal

and national governments indicate any obsession with crime, the fear of crime, the fear of victimization, or indeed, the national destiny.[14]

Crime Control

Like high levels of crime and fear of crime, punitive means of social control are taken-for-granted facts of life in the United States. Michael Milken joined more than one million Americans serving time in state and federal prisons or local jails in 1989. The United States has one of the highest recorded incarceration rates in the world. In 1993, 529 of every 100,000 Americans were in prison or jail.[15]

Levels of incarceration for selected subpopulations in the United States, particularly for socially disadvantaged groups, are even more astonishing. The incarceration rate for African-American males in the United States is higher than that in South Africa. The number of black men serving time in prison and jail in the United States is greater than the number enrolled in college. On a given day, one in every three black males between the ages of 20 and 29 is in prison or jail or on probation or parole. A 1991 study conducted by the National Center on Institutions and Alternatives found that, on any given day in Washington, D.C., over 40 percent of black males between 18 and 35 years old are either in prison or jail, on probation or parole, awaiting trial, or being sought on arrest warrants.[16] Yet, in spite of record levels of incarceration and expansions in other forms of correctional control, 85 percent of Americans believe that the courts are too lenient with criminals.[17]

Americans may worry about many things these days, but as Chapman writes, "nothing casts so large a cloud over their lives and hopes as the prevalence of violence in this country." However, if Americans take crime for granted, they badly want a remedy, and "they will latch onto anything that looks modestly promising." The perception that traditional approaches have failed and that "no one knows how to make the streets safe again" engenders a "try anything that works" attitude toward crime control.[18] In short, like crime itself, crime control in the United States is driven by a strong, at times desperate, emphasis on ends over means.

How can we explain the facts of crime and punishment that distinguish the United States from nearly all other developed nations? Has something "gone wrong" in contemporary America that accounts for high levels of crime, fear, and punitive sanctions? Or, on the contrary, is there something about the very nature of American society that generates distinctive forms and levels of crime that remain remarkably resistant to social reform and social control?

Our answer, hinted at in the previous discussion, can be stated quite simply, but its implications are far-reaching: High crime rates are intrinsic to the basic cultural commitments and institutional arrangements of American society. In short, at all social levels, America is organized for crime.

THE VIRTUES AND VICES OF THE AMERICAN DREAM

In this book, we locate the sources of crime in the very same values and behaviors that are conventionally viewed as part of the American success story. From this vantage point, high rates of crime in the United States are not the "sick" outcome of individual pathologies, such as defective personalities or aberrant biological structures. Neither are they the "evil" consequence of individual moral failings, such as greed.[19] Nor does the American crime problem simply reflect universally condemned social conditions, such as poverty and discrimination, or ineffective law enforcement, or lax punishment of criminals. Rather, crime in America derives, in significant measure, from highly prized cultural and social conditions.

The thesis of this book is that the American Dream itself and the normal social conditions engendered by it are deeply implicated in the problem of crime. In our use of the term *the American Dream,* we refer to a broad cultural ethos that entails a commitment to the goal of material success, to be pursued by everyone in society, under conditions of open, individual competition. The American Dream has both an evaluative and a cognitive dimension associated with it. People are socialized to accept the desirability of pursuing the goal of material success under the specified conditions, and they are encouraged to believe that the chances of realizing the Dream are sufficiently high to justify a continued commitment to this cultural goal. These beliefs and commitments in many respects define what it means to be an enculturated member of our society. The ethos refers quite literally to the *American* dream.

Evolution of the Concept of the American Dream

The term *the American Dream* was introduced into contemporary social analysis in 1931 by historian James Truslow Adams to describe his vision of a society open to individual achievement. Interestingly, Adams fought to have his history of the United States, *Epic of America,* entitled *The American Dream,* but his publisher rejected the idea, believing that during the Great Depression consumers would never spend $3 "on a dream."[20] The publisher clearly misread the popular mood, because the American public proved to be highly receptive to the notion of the American Dream. The term soon became a sales slogan for the material comforts and individual opportunities of a middle-class lifestyle: a car, a house, education for the children, a secure retirement.

Cultural histories of the general "success" theme in literature testify to the remarkable durability of the American Dream over the course of the twentieth century. For example, research by Charles Hearn documents the persistence of the American Dream in the popular imagination despite the profound social changes ushered in by the Great Depression. Hearn systematically reviews a wide range of literary sources published during the 1920s and 1930s, including manuals, guidebooks, and inspirational works on success, popular magazine biographies and fiction, and the fiction of highly regarded "serious" writers.

He discovers that the Great Depression altered the American Dream in subtle ways, making it more "complex, confusing, and contradictory."[21] At the same time, however, Hearn concludes that the American Dream per se was not rejected, nor was it replaced. It endured, Hearn speculates, because "the myth of success has penetrated American culture much too completely for a single crisis, even one as harrowing as the Great Depression, to deal it the death blow."[22]

The persistence of the American Dream over more recent decades is documented in the work of Elizabeth Long, who has analyzed cultural changes in the United States during the years following World War II. Long examines the shifting meanings of the dream of success as reflected in best-selling novels published between 1945 and 1975. Like Hearn, Long identifies some important changes in the collective vision of success that have occurred in response to various historical circumstances. She notes, in particular, a weakening of the commitment to an "entrepreneurial ethos"—that is, an ethos according to which the pursuit of individual self-interest necessarily promotes social progress. Significantly, her study does not extend to the "Reagan revolution" of the 1980s and the consolidation of the conservative agenda in the 1990s, which rehabilitated the idea that the self-interested pursuit of economic success promotes the common good. In any event, Long emphasizes that the core components of the American Dream were reflected in popular writing throughout the thirty-year period following World War II, and she concludes that no new cultural ethos has emerged to replace the traditional view of success.[23]

The salience of the American Dream in the public consciousness is also reflected in the extent to which this term continues to permeate discourse about success in the contemporary literature. In a computer search of book titles with the key words *American* and *dream,* we discovered over a hundred titles in the holdings of the University of Missouri library system. These titles covered topics as diverse as "baseball and the American Dream," "talk radio and the American Dream," "LSD and the American Dream," and "zoning and the American Dream." In short, today as in the past, the dream of individual material success continues to captivate the popular imagination in the United States, and it serves as a cultural compass guiding Americans in their everyday lives.

The Dark Side of the American Dream

The strong and persistent appeal of the American Dream has without question been highly beneficial for our society. The commitments associated with this cultural ethos have provided the motivational dynamic for economic expansion, extraordinary technological innovation, and high rates of social mobility. But there is a paradoxical quality to the American Dream. The very features that are responsible for the impressive accomplishments of American society have less desirable consequences as well. The American Dream is a mixed blessing, contributing to both the best and the worst elements of the American character and society. In the words of sociologist Robert K. Merton, "a cardinal American virtue, 'ambition,' promotes a cardinal American vice, 'deviant behavior.'"[24]

The cultural emphasis on achievement, which promotes productivity and innovation, also generates pressures to succeed at any cost. The glorification of individual competition, which fosters ambition and mobility, drives people apart and weakens the collective sense of community. Finally, the preoccupation with monetary rewards, which undergirds economic demand in a market economy, severely restricts the kinds of achievements to which people are motivated to aspire.

Monetary Success and Noneconomic Roles   The exaggerated priority given to *monetary* rewards has particularly important ramifications for the cultural valuation placed on roles performed in noneconomic contexts. Tasks that are primarily noneconomic in nature tend to receive meager cultural support, and the skillful performance of these tasks elicits little public recognition. Consider the meaning of education in America. A "good" education has historically been part of the middle-class success package. However, education has been viewed primarily as a means to an end. The image of "a good student" as an intrinsically worthy ideal is missing from the portrait of the American Dream. Nor do Americans accord much respect to teachers, as reflected in the old adage "Those who can, do; those who can't, teach."[25]

Similar dynamics can be observed within the realm of the family. A "devoted parent" occupies a rather tenuous position in the American Dream. This devotion is commonly understood in terms of the capacity to provide "a better life" or "a chance to get ahead"—that is, opportunities for economic success—for one's children. The comments by Marian Wright Edelman, head of the Children's Defense Fund, are very illuminating in this regard. Observing recent increases in the poverty rates of children in families headed by parents younger than thirty, Edelman speculates that "raising and nurturing children may no longer be compatible with active pursuit of the American dream."[26] We would qualify Edelman's remarks by noting that "nurturing children" per se has never been a significant component of the American Dream, even during good times.

Also relevant for our purposes, a concern with citizenship and the performance of political roles for the furtherance of the collective good is conspicuously absent from the American Dream. The cultural emphasis is on individual success, and the role of government is conceived of largely in terms of its capacity to facilitate individual material advancement. In short, the materialistic element of the American Dream emphasizes achievements in one exclusive domain of social life and implicitly devalues achievements and performances in all others. In so doing, the American Dream generates exceptionally strong pressures to succeed in a narrowly defined way and to pursue such success by the technically most efficient means, that is, by any means necessary.

Universalism and Economic Inequality   Another feature of the American Dream that has paradoxical implications is its *universalism*. All Americans, regardless of social origins or social location, are encouraged to embrace the tenets of the dominant cultural ethos. The imperative to succeed, or at least to keep on trying to succeed, respects no social boundaries. This universalism of goals is in many respects a matter of pride for Americans. It reflects an under-lying democratic ethos and a belief in a common entitlement for everyone in society. Yet this universal application of monetary success goals inevitably cre-ates serious dilemmas for large numbers of individuals in a social structure characterized by appreciable economic inequality. Because the culture pre-cludes the possibility of noncompeting groups, and because it assigns higher priority to monetary success than to other goals, the status of being economi-cally "unequal" is readily equated with being "unsuccessful" and, by extension, "unworthy."

It might thus seem reasonable to expect that the universalism inherent in the American Dream is naturally conducive to egalitarian social structures. Ac-cordingly, the current level of inequality in the United States might be viewed as something of an aberration, a temporary mismatch between culture and so-cial structure—a betrayal of the American Dream.[27] At first glance, evidence seems to support such a position. Economic inequalities have in fact grown in recent years. For example, the share of income received by the poorest fifth of American families dropped from 5.2 percent in 1980 to 4.2 percent in 1993. The share received by the richest fifth increased from 41.5 percent to 46.2 percent over the same period. The distribution of wealth (assets in the form of home mortgages and other real estate, businesses, bank accounts, stocks, bonds, and other securities) has also taken what two economists have termed a "great U-turn" toward growing inequality.[28]

However, recent changes in economic inequality should not obscure the more fundamental *stability* that has characterized the distribution of income and wealth in the United States over time. The poorest fifth of families and unattached individuals has consistently received about 5 percent and the rich-est fifth between 40 and 45 percent of total income for nearly a half century. According to one economist:

> Family income inequality is very large, but it has remained relatively con-stant since World War II. There have been some trends: a drift toward equality through the late 1960s; a drift away from equality through the 1970s; a slightly sharper move from equality since 1979. But these move-ments have been modest.[29]

The distribution of wealth is even more concentrated than the distribution of income, and it shows striking historical stability. The available data are rough, but it appears that the richest 1 percent of the U.S. population has owned some-where between 20 and 36 percent of all assets in America since 1820.[30] In other words, in spite of (1) massive shifts in the occupational structure, (2) the movement of the population from farm to city to suburb, (3) booms and busts in the business cycle, (4) Republican and Democratic administrations, and (5) a host of governmental interventions and regulations, the American economic structure has been consistently characterized by substantial inequality.

A particularly important aspect of inequality in American society concerns the economic circumstances of children. In this regard the United States stands apart from other developed nations. A comparison of eighteen advanced industrial nations conducted by the Luxembourg Income Study indicates that the gap between the average income of the richest and poorest deciles of households with children is widest in the United States. In addition, the United States also has more limited social programs such as medical and child care services. Were these noncash benefits taken into account, the contrast between the United States and the other nations would be even greater.[31]

We suggest that the extreme and persistent economic inequality in the United States is best understood not as a departure from fundamental cultural orientations but rather as an expression of them. Despite the universalistic component of the American Dream, the basic logic of this cultural ethos actually *presupposes* high levels of inequality. A competitive allocation of monetary rewards requires both winners and losers, and winning and losing have meaning only when rewards are distributed unequally. The motivation to endure the competitive struggle is not maintained easily if the monetary difference between winning and losing is inconsequential. In short, a fundamental tension is built into the very fabric of the American Dream. It provides the cultural foundation for a high level of economic inequality, yet a high level of inequality relegates large segments of the population to the role of "failure" as defined by the standards of the very same cultural ethos.

The American Dream thus has a dark side that must be considered in any serious effort to uncover the social sources of crime. It encourages an exaggerated emphasis on monetary achievements while devaluing alternative criteria of success, it promotes a preoccupation with the realization of goals while deemphasizing the importance of the ways in which these goals are pursued, and it helps create and sustain social structures incapable of restraining criminogenic cultural pressures.

The general idea that crime is produced by many of the same features of American society that also contribute to its successes is not new. This notion, which can be termed the "criminogenic hypothesis," was part of the critical social problems literature that emerged in the United States during the 1960s. A good example of this social criticism is Edwin Schur's provocative *Our Criminal Society,* published in 1969. A more recent example of a critical work that attributes crime to a "wilding culture" presumed to be associated with the American Dream is Charles Derber's *Money, Murder and the American Dream.*[32] However, as shown in Chapter 4, our explanation of crime is only superficially similar to such accounts of crime as a "social problem." The intellectual roots of our orientation are to be found not in contemporary critiques of American society but in the classical sociological analyses of Émile Durkheim and Robert K. Merton, specifically in their analyses of social deviance and "anomie."

THE RISE, FALL, AND REVIVAL OF THE ANOMIE PERSPECTIVE

Core Ideas, Assumptions, and Propositions

The French sociologist Émile Durkheim, a founding figure in sociology, directed attention in the late nineteenth century to the critical role of social factors in explaining human behavior. He also introduced the term *anomie* to refer to a weakening of the normative order in society, and he explored in some detail the consequences of anomie for suicide, a form of deviant behavior that typically is explained with reference to psychological factors.[33]

Our analysis is grounded in the variant of anomie theory associated with the work of the American sociologist Robert K. Merton. Merton combines strategic ideas from Durkheim with insights borrowed from Karl Marx, another founding figure in the social sciences, to produce a provocative and compelling account of the social forces underlying deviant behavior in American society. Although we go beyond Merton's thesis in several important respects (as explained more fully in Chapters 3 and 4), we nevertheless borrow liberally from his arguments and from the anomie research program in sociology and criminology.

Most importantly, we accept Merton's underlying premise that motivations for crime do not result simply from the flaws, failures, or free choices of individuals. A complete explanation of crime ultimately must consider the sociocultural environments in which people are located. Similar to motivations and desires that promote conformity to norms, deviant and criminal motivations cannot be predicted solely on the basis of assumptions about the "native drives" of the human species.[34] They must be explained, instead, with reference to the particular cultural settings in which people conduct their daily lives. The cultural conditioning of human motivations and desires has been expressed very nicely by Schopenhauer: "We want what we will, but we don't will what we want."[35]

We also find considerable merit in the observation, basic to both Merton's and Marx's sociological analysis, that strains, tensions, and contradictions are built into concrete forms of social organization. These internal contradictions ultimately provide the impetus for change, and they help account for the dynamic aspects of collective social life.[36] Undesirable forms of behavior, such as crime, thus may be inevitable features of the normal workings of the social system, just as are more desirable forms of behavior. Crime does not have to be understood as the product of mysterious or bizarre forces; it can be viewed as an ordinary and predictable response to prevailing sociocultural conditions.[37]

Merton argues that the United States is a prime example of a social system characterized by internal strain and contradictions. Specifically, Merton observes that an exaggerated emphasis is placed on the goal of monetary success in American society coupled with a weak emphasis placed on the importance of using the socially acceptable means for achieving this goal. This is a normal feature of American culture; as we suggested earlier, it is an integral part of the American Dream. In addition, access to the legitimate means for attaining success is unequally distributed across the social structure. The result of these cultural and structural conditions is a pronounced strain toward anomie, that is, a tendency for social norms to lose their regulatory force. Merton suggests that this anomic quality of life is responsible for the high rates of crime and deviance characteristic of the United States. He also proposes that similar sociocultural processes account for the social distribution of crime. The pressures toward anomie, according to Merton, are socially structured. They become progressively more intense at lower levels of the social class hierarchy, because obstacles to the use of the legitimate means for success are greater in the lower classes.

The "Golden Age" of Anomie Theory

Merton's version of anomie theory was introduced to the scholarly community in an article entitled "Social Structure and Anomie," originally published in the *American Sociological Review* in 1938. This article had little immediate impact on the fields of criminology and the sociology of deviance. As one commentator, Stephen Pfohl, has observed, the "essay sat dormant for about fifteen years after its first publication."[38] Then, in the 1950s, anomie theory began to capture the imagination of influential theorists and researchers. Ambiguities in the original statement of the theory were identified and remedies proposed. Prominent sociologists and criminologists integrated aspects of anomie theory with other criminological ideas to construct explanations of crime and deviance that were both more comprehensive and more precise than Merton's original formulation. The most noteworthy of these efforts were Albert Cohen's *Delinquent Boys* and Richard Cloward and Lloyd Ohlin's *Delinquency and Opportunity.*

Cohen extends Merton's theory to explain how delinquent subcultures emerged from reactions by working-class youth to the middle-class success norms of the school. Cloward and Ohlin join Merton's theory with the "differential association" perspective on crime developed by Edwin Sutherland to explain how different forms of criminal and deviant activity, including the activities commonly associated with urban youth gangs, result from the failure of lower-class youth to achieve economic success in both the legitimate and the illegitimate "opportunity structures" of the contemporary city.[39] These extensions of Merton's theory highlight the ways in which basic structural conditions can generate subcultures conducive to criminal motivations, thereby explaining the social distribution of crime within a society. Merton himself further advanced the anomie research program by responding to early criticisms of his original theoretical statement and offering expanded and revised versions of the theory in a series of subsequent publications in 1959, 1964, and 1968.[40]

In addition to a growing interest in the theoretical structure of Merton's argument, a large number of empirical studies informed by anomie theory appeared in the late 1950s and throughout the 1960s. The theory was applied to a wide range of deviant behaviors, including crime, delinquency, drug addiction, mental illness, and alcoholism. Researchers interested in macrolevel analysis proposed objective indicators of anomie to explain aggregate crime rates, whereas those interested in individual-level analysis developed social psychological scales of the subjective experience of confronting an "anomic" environment.[41]

The overall influence of the anomie perspective on the sociological study of deviance during the middle years of the twentieth century is difficult to overstate. In the 1992 edition of his widely used criminology textbook, Don Gibbons proclaims that the body of ideas associated with the anomie perspective has served as "the most influential formulation on the sociology of deviance over the past fifty years, as attested by the copious citations . . . in sociological textbooks."[42] Jonathan Turner offers a similar assessment in his text on sociological theory, suggesting that probably no single sociological essay published in this century has prompted as much research and theoretical commentary as Merton's "Social Structure and Anomie."[43] The impact of anomie theory has not been limited to the academic community. Major policy initiatives such as the Mobilization for Youth Program in the 1960s and the War on Poverty more generally were heavily indebted to the general ideas associated with the anomie perspective.[44]

Decline and Revival

Interest in anomie theory, however, dropped markedly in the 1970s and 1980s. Researchers were less likely to draw on the anomie perspective for theoretical guidance, as reflected in the declining number of citations to Merton's work beginning in the early 1970s.[45] In addition, several highly respected scholars directed harsh criticisms at the anomie perspective. In an influential monograph on juvenile delinquency published in 1978, Ruth Kornhauser dismisses the utility of "strain theory," the label given to anomie theory by criminological theorists in the 1970s, on both theoretical and empirical grounds. She argues that the theory suffers from grievous logical flaws and that its central empirical claims (for example, that the discrepancy between aspirations and achievements is a cause of delinquency) lack support in the research literature. Kornhauser concludes her review of the perspective with the blunt advice to colleagues to turn their attention elsewhere in efforts to explain crime and delinquency.[46]

Anomie theory came under fire from a number of theoretical positions in the 1970s and 1980s, but it would be a mistake to attribute its declining stature during that time to any definitive disconfirmation of its principal claims or to the emergence of a clearly superior alternative. Theoretical dominance in social science reflects not only the intrinsic merits of perspectives but also broader social and political conditions. As the liberal consensus that characterized the postwar era in the United States weakened in the late 1970s, as the welfare state and antipoverty programs came under political fire during the early years of the Reagan administration, as the social movements that provided the political pressure for social welfare policies disappeared, and as crime rates continued to climb, the necessary social supports for a theory universally regarded as advocating liberal social reform as a way to reduce crime withered away.[47]

The anomie perspective appears, however, to be enjoying a resurgence of interest in criminology. This is reflected in critical reviews of the earlier critiques, original empirical research applying the perspective, and efforts to elaborate the general theory.[48] Perhaps part of the reason for the renewed interest in anomie theory is the return of an intellectual climate more receptive to its major premises and claims. Given the growing awareness of vexing contemporary social problems—such as homelessness, the urban underclass, persistent economic stagnation accompanied by glaring social inequalities, and urban decay in general—explanations of social behavior cast in terms of fundamental characteristics of society, rather than individual deficiencies, are likely once again to "make sense" to many criminologists.[49]

Regardless of the extent to which anomie theory is in tune with the general intellectual climate, we maintain that this theoretical perspective warrants renewed attention in its own right. The diagnosis of the crime problem advanced by Merton in the 1930s remains highly relevant to contemporary conditions. The most valuable and insightful feature of the anomie perspective, in our view, is that it treats as problematic those enduring cultural and social conditions that liberals and conservatives alike view as potential solutions for crime, such as economic growth, a renewed "competitiveness," and greater equality of opportunity—in short, a renewed commitment to the American Dream.[50]

Unfinished Business

The anomie perspective as developed by Merton and his followers does not, however, provide a fully comprehensive sociological explanation of crime in America. The most glaring limitation of Merton's analysis is that it focuses exclusively on one aspect of social structure: inequality in access to the legitimate means for success. As a consequence, it does not explain how specific features of the broader *institutional structure* of society, beyond the stratification system, interrelate to produce the anomic pressures that are responsible for crime.

Anomie theory is thus best regarded as a work in progress. In the words of Albert Cohen, an influential proponent of the anomie perspective: "Merton has laid the groundwork for an explanation of deviance [and crime] on the sociological level, but the task, for the most part, still lies ahead."[51] In the pages that follow, we begin to address the task to which Cohen refers. We explicate the interconnections between culture and institutional structure in contemporary American society, and then explore the implications of these interconnections for crime and for efforts at crime control. Before introducing our explanatory framework, it is necessary to describe in greater detail the nature of the crime problem in American society.

NOTES

1. Eichenwald (1990); Stewart (1991, p. 415). The $318,000 estimate of the cost of Milken's misdeeds is reported in Dershowitz (1992).

2. Truell (1995); *New York Times* (1990a).

3. For Milken's view of his mission of economic "reform," see the opinion piece by Michael Lewis (1990); on Milken's "legacy," see *New York Times* (1990b); on Milken's reduced sentence, see Sullivan (1992).

4. Clines (1993, p. 7).

5. Berke (1993, p. A12); Bradsher (1990).

6. Erikson (1966, p. 21).

7. The scenarios are from case file summaries for 1985–1989. See Rosenfeld (1991) for a description of data collection and coding procedures.

8. Black (1984); on crime as a form of social control in illegal markets, see Reuter (1984).

9. The U.S. homicide total for 1990 is from the Federal Bureau of Investigation (1991). Comparative data on crime for the United States and other developed nations are presented in Chapter 2. For further cross-national comparisons of crime rates, see Archer and Gartner (1984); Dobrin, Wiersema, Loftin, and McDowall (1996).

10. Data for Scotland are from World Health Organization (1994); St. Louis data are from Federal Bureau of Investigation (1993b).

11. The percentages have been calculated by the authors from the General Social Survey (GSS) data for 1994 using the MicroCase analysis program. GSS data are from annual surveys of nationally representative samples of American adults conducted by the National Opinion Research Center.

12. Marriott (1995).

13. For evidence concerning fear of crime and neighborhood satisfaction, see Skogan (1990, pp. 83–84). The reference to the Rodney King case in Los Angeles is from Chapman (1992). In a subsequent federal trial, two of the police officers in this case were found guilty of violating King's civil rights.

14. Adler (1983, p. xix).

15. Bureau of Justice Statistics (1995b, p. 2). See Mauer (1991) for international comparisons.

16. National data for black males are from Mauer and Huling (1995) and Mortenson (1996). See Miller (1992) for a description of the Washington study. See Bureau of Justice Statistics (1995a) for data on recent expansions in correctional control in the United States.

17. Calculated by the authors from 1994 GSS data.

18. Chapman (1992).

19. For a general discussion of the view that "evil" outcomes must have "evil" causes and of alternative perspectives, see Nisbet (1971, pp. 9–14).

20. Adams (1931) has been referred to as "the historian of the American Dream" by his biographer Allan Nevins (1968; see p. 68n for the reference to the publisher's resistance to Adams's preferred title).

21. Hearn (1977, pp. 18, 192).

22. Hearn (1977, p. 201).

23. Long (1985, p. 196).

24. Merton (1968, p. 200).

25. This adage is invoked in a similar context by Schwartz (1994b, p. 259) in his discussion of the "debasing of education."

26. Quoted in *St. Louis Post-Dispatch* (1992b).

27. See Ropers (1991) for an analysis that attributes persistent poverty to the "American Dream Turned Nightmare."

28. Statistics on income distribution are from the U.S. Bureau of the Census (1995, p. 475, Table 733). The reference for the "great U-turn" is Harrison and Bluestone (1988, pp. 135–138).

29. Levy (1988, p. 2); see also Turner and Musick (1985, p. 178).

30. Turner and Musick (1985, p. 181). For documentation of recent growth in the concentration of wealth, see Wolff (1995). Schwarz (1995/96) discusses the historical stability of economic inequality in the United States.

31. Bradsher (1995).

32. Schur (1969); Derber (1992, 1996).

33. Durkheim ([1893] 1964a; [1897] 1966).

34. Merton (1968, p. 175).

35. Quoted in Johnson (1991, p. 26).

36. Merton (1968, p. 176).

37. See Orru (1990, p. 232).

38. Merton (1938); Pfohl (1985, p. 226).

39. Cohen (1955); Cloward and Ohlin (1960); see also Lilly, Cullen, and Ball (1989), pp. 71–75. The central premise of differential association theory is that people learn criminal motivations and behaviors through exposure to norms and beliefs that favor law violation. See Sutherland (1947) for an early statement of the perspective and Chapter 3 for an expanded discussion and critique of Sutherland's theory.

40. Merton (1959, 1964, 1968).

41. See Clinard (1964) for an appraisal of early work in these areas.

42. Gibbons (1992, p. 110).

43. Turner (1978, p. 83).

44. Liska (1987, pp. 51–54).

45. Cole (1975).

46. Kornhauser (1978, p. 180).

47. Material in this paragraph is drawn from Rosenfeld (1989).

48. See, for example, Agnew (1992), Bernard (1984), Farnworth and Lieber (1989), Menard (1995), Messner (1988), and Volume 6 of *Advances in Criminological Theory*, which is devoted to "the legacy of anomie" (Adler and Laufer 1995).

49. See Lilly et al. (1989, pp. 77, 81).

50. See Samuelson (1992) for an insightful discussion of the widespread belief that prosperity is a panacea for social problems.

51. Cohen (1985, p. 233).

2

By Any Means Necessary: Serious Crime in America

It is needless to waste words in painting the situation in our country today. The headlines of any metropolitan newspaper any day do so only too clearly. Crime of the most desperate sort is so rampant that unless a robbery runs into six figures or a murder is outstandingly brutal or intriguing, we no longer even read below the headings.

JAMES TRUSLOW ADAMS,
HISTORIAN, 1929

I miss crime, murder. I haven't heard about any good shootings or stabbings. I miss Philadelphia.

CHARLES BARKLEY,
PROFESSIONAL BASKETBALL PLAYER

Charles Barkley's joking reference during the 1992 summer Olympic Games to the American crime problem is a blunt reminder that serious crime is viewed throughout the world as a normal, if undesirable, feature of American society. It is difficult to envision athletes from any other nation joking in this way about crime and violence in their homeland. Stabbings and shootings would not be accepted as laughably routine events in London, Stockholm, Oslo, Paris, or Bombay. Yet Barkley's crime joke provoked little criticism from the American press (outside Philadelphia), which seemed more concerned with the size of the "dream team's" victory margins over other nations than with the size of the crime rates in U.S. cities.[1]

Barkley's joke about missing the violence in Philadelphia may be faulted for being in poor taste, but it nevertheless is rooted in objective social reality, as were James Truslow Adams's observations at the end of the 1920s quoted at the beginning of this chapter. Violent acts such as shootings and stabbings occur in American cities with alarming frequency. To illustrate: 444 homicides,

904 rapes, 7,280 aggravated assaults, and 13,921 robberies—a total of 22,549 violent crimes—were reported to the Philadelphia police during the year before the 1992 summer Olympics. Three hundred nineteen, or 72 percent, of the murders were committed with a gun; another sixty-seven involved a knife or other cutting instrument. Guns or knives were used in well over half of the 7,280 aggravated assaults.[2]

To appreciate fully the social significance of these figures, it is useful to express them in terms of the average person's risk for becoming a crime victim. With Philadelphia's population of just over 1.5 million in 1991, the average Philadelphia resident stood a 1-in-70 chance of becoming a victim of a violent crime in that year. This is undoubtedly a very conservative estimate of the risk of violent crime faced by Philadelphians, because half of the violent crimes (excluding homicides) committed in the United States are not reported to the police. According to estimates from the National Crime Victimization Survey (NCVS), 49 percent of robbery, rape, and assault victimizations nationwide in 1991 were reported to the police.[3] Assuming that Philadelphians report crimes to the police at about the rate for the nation as a whole, the actual risk of becoming a victim of a violent crime during a single year in Philadelphia is therefore closer to 1 in 35.

Although he singled out Philadelphia, Barkley could have invoked the violent reputation of almost any large American city in his commentary on crime in the United States. In fact, rates of serious crime tend to be somewhat lower in Philadelphia than in many other large cities. In 1990, Philadelphia's murder rate of thirty-two murders for every 100,000 residents fell considerably below the murder rates in Detroit, New Orleans, St. Louis, and Atlanta, the site of the 1996 summer Olympic games. The murder rate in Philadelphia was less than half of that in Washington, D.C., which led the nation in homicides per capita in 1990, winning the dubious distinction as the nation's "murder capital." Rates of nonlethal violent crimes also are lower in Philadelphia than in many other large American cities. Among the nation's fifty largest cities in 1990, Philadelphia ranked forty-fifth in rapes, nineteenth in robberies, and fortieth in assaults per capita.[4]

In view of the pervasiveness of violent crime throughout urban America, and not merely in the "City of Brotherly Love," it is easy for Americans to suppose that criminal violence is an inevitable feature of modern, industrial society. However, this understandable supposition runs directly counter to a leading theoretical perspective and a sizeable research literature on long-term trends in crime rates. This body of work, referred to as the *modernization thesis,* reveals that Western societies exhibit levels of interpersonal violence today that are considerably lower than they were centuries ago. To explain this long-term decline in interpersonal violence, historian Ted Robert Gurr offers the idea of a "civilizing process" (an idea originally introduced by Norbert Elias). As Western civilization has progressed, Gurr argues, internal and external controls on the overt display of violence have increased markedly, and humanistic values have become more widely accepted.[5]

The relationship between modernization and crime also has been explored in quantitative, cross-sectional analyses based on samples of contemporary nations at varying stages of development. Consistent with the historical research, cross-sectional studies provide no support for the notion that a high level of criminal violence is a natural feature of the social landscape of modern industrial societies.[6] The question prompted by comparisons of the "developed" societies of the world is not why rates of serious crime are consistently high across all or most of them, but rather why they are so exceptionally high in one of them: the United States. This is the basic question about crime that we address in this book.

In the present chapter, we review the available international statistics on two of the most serious types of conventional crime: robbery and homicide. We then consider evidence about the extent of white-collar crime in the United States. Although reliable estimates of the volume of this kind of offending are not available for international comparisons, clear evidence indicates that white-collar crime is widespread and costly. Moreover, both types of crime—"suite" crime as well as "street" crime—have devastating consequences for both those who are victimized and those who live in fear of becoming crime victims.

Chapter 2 closes with qualitative descriptions drawn from news accounts of how individuals and communities cope with conditions that in many respects parallel those during wartime. In their portrayal of personal struggles with crime and fear, the vignettes put a human face on the official statistics on crime in America. These descriptions also reveal an institutional struggle with crime in many American communities, as businesses, churches, schools, and families find themselves under siege and, in their weakened condition, end up contributing to even higher levels of neighborhood disorganization and crime. This focus on the interplay between crime and social institutions sets the stage for the assessment and reformulation of sociological explanations of crime in Chapter 3.

CROSS-NATIONAL
COMPARISONS OF CRIME

Robbery and Homicide Rates in International Context

Comparisons of the crime rates of different nations must be viewed with considerable caution. Both the reporting of crimes to the police and police recording practices differ from one nation to another, as do procedures for reporting crime statistics to international agencies. Most importantly, different nations employ differing definitions of crime. Although these problems are less likely to affect comparisons across developed nations of the most serious offenses, such as those under consideration here, it is best to treat small differences in crime rates between nations as unreliable, especially when comparisons are based on data for a single year.[7]

In any event, the differences of interest for our purposes, namely, those between the United States and other advanced industrial nations, are anything

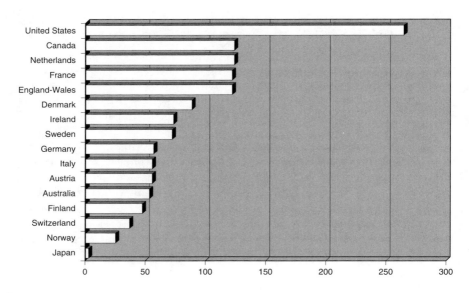

FIGURE 2–1 Robbery Rates in Sixteen Nations, 1992 (robberies per 100,000 population)

but small. Rates of serious predatory crime are unquestionably greater in the United States. Figures 2–1 and 2–2 compare the 1992 U.S. robbery and homicide rates, respectively, with those of fifteen other industrial nations. The data on robbery rates are from the International Police Organization, which defines robbery as "violent theft." This definition accords with the general classification of robberies in the United States and elsewhere as thefts (including attempts) accompanied by force or the threat of force. The homicide data are from the World Health Organization, which defines homicide as "death by injury purposely inflicted by others."[8]

Figure 2–1 vividly displays the marked difference between the U.S. robbery rate and those of other developed nations. The U.S. rate of 264 robberies per 100,000 residents is more than twice as high as the rates in the nations with the next highest rates, Canada and the Netherlands. It is almost 150 times the robbery rate in Japan, which reported 1.8 robberies per 100,000 population in 1992, the lowest rate of any of the nations depicted in Figure 2–1.

The relative differences between the rate of homicide in the United States and those of other developed nations are even greater than the differences in robbery rates. The U.S. rate of 10.0 homicides per 100,000 population is approximately three times Finland's rate of 3.4 per 100,000 population, the next highest among the nations presented in Figure 2–2; it is over seven times the rates of most of the other nations. Although several recent shootings in Japan have prompted concerns about an "Americanization of crime" there, with a rate of less than one homicide for every 100,000 residents, Japan is in no

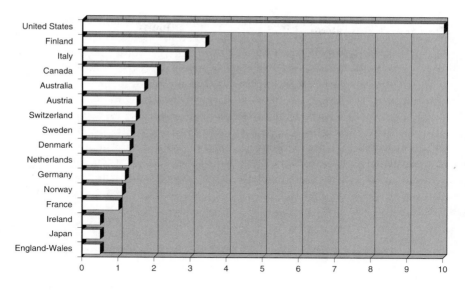

FIGURE 2–2 Homicide Rates in Sixteen Nations, 1992 (homicides per 100,000 population)

immediate danger of catching the United States in this particular area of international comparison.[9]

The case for American exceptionalism in crime should not be overstated. Some nations exhibit homicide rates that exceed those of the United States. For example, South Africa was designated the "murder capital of the world" by the World Health Organization in 1995, and in the years following the break-up of the former Soviet Union, homicide rates in the Russian Federation have surpassed those of the United States.[10] Nevertheless, when it comes to lethal violence, America clearly stands out as one of the leaders of the modern world.

It is also important to note that rates for certain property crimes are not exceptionally high in the United States, although it is usually at or near the top in comparisons of advanced societies.[11] However, when comparing the crime situation across nations, we must consider the form of criminal activity along with its level. What seems to be most distinctive about property crime in the United States is its unrestrained and dangerous character. It is more likely to take the form, in other words, of illegal activity "by any means necessary." This is reflected in the robbery statistics reported earlier. Robbery is technically defined in the United States and other countries as a violent offense, but it is a crime whose primary objective is the acquisition of property. Indeed, one might think of robbery as theft by any means necessary.

An amusing and instructive illustration of ways in which property crimes might differ across societies in form, even if not in frequency, is provided by David Bayley in his analysis of the role of "propriety" in Japanese society.[12]

Bayley cites the case of a burglar who was apprehended fleeing an apartment. The burglar was caught because he had stopped to put his shoes on. Why did he have his shoes off in the first place? In Japan, it is customary to remove one's shoes when entering a private home, especially if the home has the traditional flooring of woven straw. The burglar had to cross such a floor to get at a bureau that he wanted to ransack; thus, in accordance with Japanese notions of propriety, he first removed his shoes. Evidently, the Japanese sense of propriety affects even the way burglars conduct their illegal activities. It is hard to imagine the typical American burglar exhibiting similar restraint when committing his or her crimes. Of course, Swedish or Canadian burglars may also find the Japanese sense of propriety in crime somewhat demanding. However, the general point is consistent with the cross-national evidence on crime: the more serious the offense, the greater the actual or potential harm to the victim, and the more unrestrained its character, the more the United States diverges from other advanced industrial societies.

Gun-Related Crime

An important question underlying the commanding predominance of the United States over other industrial nations in serious crime involves the use of firearms: How much of the difference in crime rates is accounted for by the greater availability of guns in the United States? Rates of gun ownership are much higher in America than in other industrial nations. A 1989 crime victimization survey of fourteen developed nations found that 29 percent of U.S. households contained a handgun. Switzerland, where handguns were reported in 14 percent of all households, had the second highest rate of handgun ownership. It is important to recognize, however, that just over one-half of these firearms were owned by Swiss males in their capacity as members of the army. No other nation in the survey had a handgun ownership rate higher than 7 percent.[13]

Although most homicides in the United States are committed with a gun, and most gun-related homicides are committed with a handgun, it is difficult to determine precisely how much of the U.S. homicide rate can be attributed to the widespread availability of firearms.[14] For our purposes such a determination is unnecessary, however, because even if all of the gun-related homicides were eliminated from its homicide rate, the United States would still have a *nongun* homicide rate that is higher than the total homicide rates of most other developed nations.

We can illustrate this point with some simple calculations. In 1992, 68 percent of the homicides in the United States were committed with a gun. The remaining 32 percent were committed with other weapons (usually a knife) or without a weapon. Therefore, the nongun homicide rate in the United States was 32 percent of the total rate (32 percent $\times$ 10.0), or 3.2 per 100,000 population.[15] This level of lethal violence committed without a firearm is greater than the overall homicide rates of all but one of the other nations displayed in Figure 2–2 and, in most cases, considerably greater. For example, it is more than five times the 1992 rate for England and Wales of 0.6 homicides per 100,000 population. As in many other nations, British law and custom strongly discourage the private ownership of firearms. Yet even if no homicides in England and Wales were committed with a firearm, restricted access to guns could not explain the sizeable difference between the American nongun homicide rate and the total homicide rate in Britain. As a British gun control analyst is reported to have quipped:

> Since America so greatly exceeds England not just in the rate of gun crime but in that with knives, should we assume that butcher knives are illegal in England? And if more guns explain the much higher U.S. gun crime rates, what explains the much higher rates of unarmed Americans robbing or beating each other to death: Do Americans have more hands and feet than Britons?[16]

We are not proposing that the huge supply of guns in the United States—which at over 200 million amounts to the largest private arsenal in the world—has no bearing on its rate of lethal violence. We simply want to call attention to the equally sobering point that even if none of these weapons were ever used in another killing, the United States would still be left with one of the highest rates of homicide among the advanced industrial nations.

A tragic illustration of the cultural complexities underlying the guns–crime relationship is the response of the Japanese public when, on Halloween night in 1992, a sixteen-year-old exchange student from Japan was shot to death by a homeowner near Baton Rouge, Louisiana. The student knocked on the door of a house where he mistakenly thought a party was being held. He was shot when he continued to approach the owner, apparently not understanding the command to "freeze." The Japanese were shocked by the killing itself. Many were even more appalled, however, by the subsequent acquittal of the American homeowner on the grounds of self-defense. In the words of a professor of American cultural studies at the University of Tokyo: "I think for the Japanese the most remarkable thing is that you could get a jury of Americans together, and they could conclude that shooting someone before you even talked to him was reasonable behavior."[17]

This account suggests that the Japanese do not attribute the killing of the exchange student, and presumably other homicides in the United States, simply to the availability of firearms. Rather, they look to deeper cultural differences for an explanation of the striking contrast between Japan and America in both the number of lethal weapons in private hands and the level of interpersonal violence. Japanese commentators characterized the events surrounding the killing, the plea of "self-defense" against an unarmed teenager in a Halloween costume, and the jury's verdict of not guilty, as a reflection of an "out-of-control" society in which people are allowed to shoot one another with little or no provocation. According to the American studies professor quoted earlier, the cultural significance of the Baton Rouge case is that Americans and Japanese "go by different rules." "We are more civilized," she concludes. "We rely on words."

One does not have to endorse the invidious claim that the Japanese are "more civilized" to concur with the general sentiment expressed in these remarks that the exceptional level of lethal violence in the United States involves something more than the quantity, availability, or lethality of firearms. An adequate explanation of gun-related violence must account for those qualities of the cultural "rules" that make Americans unusually willing to deploy the means of final resort in dealing with perceived threats and interpersonal disputes.

Has It Always Been This Way?

Another question raised by international crime comparisons is whether the exceptionally high rates observed for the United States are relatively recent in origin or have persisted over a long period of time. This issue has sparked some disagreement among scholars concerning the impact of modernization on crime rates in the United States. Louise Shelley addresses the "anomaly" of persistently high levels of crime in American society as follows:

> The crime patterns of the United States are unique among all developed countries in terms of the high rates of criminal behavior, the pervasiveness of the phenomenon, and the severity of the crimes that are committed. The country has not benefited from the stabilization in crime patterns that appears to accompany the maturation of the developmental process.[18]

In contrast, Ted Robert Gurr offers a more qualified assessment of the extent to which the United States diverges from the downward trend in violence evidenced in other industrial societies and expected on the basis of the modernization thesis. In a discussion of three major increases in violent crime over the last two centuries in the United States, Gurr suggests that these "waves are of such amplitude that we cannot say conclusively whether they are superimposed on a long-run decline."[19]

On one point, however, there is little debate among crime historians: Since the beginning of the twentieth century and perhaps as far back as the middle of the nineteenth century, violent crime rates in the United States have far exceeded those in other modern industrial societies. The persistence of comparatively high levels of homicide in the United States is documented in Figure 2–3 for the period 1900–1993.[20] Two observations are apparent in Figure 2–3 regarding change and persistence in levels of homicide in the United States during the twentieth century. The first is the considerable variability in homicide rates over the period. The level of homicide more than doubled during the first decades of the century, peaking at over nine homicides per 100,000 population in the early 1930s. Homicide rates then declined to under five per 100,000 population during the 1950s and early 1960s. They then began a second period of pronounced increase, comparable to that at the beginning of the century. The second observation to be made about these changes, however, is that they occur around a high and apparently stationary base rate. The mean level of homicide of just under seven per 100,000 population is not

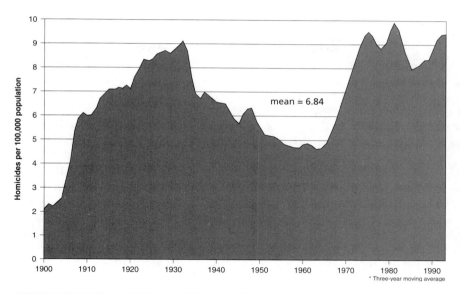

FIGURE 2–3 U.S. Homicide Rates, 1990–1993 (three-year moving average)

simply inflated by the very high rates of recent decades; it also reflects the elevated rates of earlier decades in the century.

Although comparative time-series data are limited, the mean level of homicide during the twentieth century in the United States substantially exceeds the highest rates of other industrial nations. In fact, with few exceptions, the lowest annual rates of homicide recorded in the United States over the past ninety years are greater than the highest rates found in other industrial societies.[21] Although the temporal comparisons cannot be definitive, it seems reasonably clear that the exceptionally high level of homicide in the United States observed in Figure 2–2 is not a recent phenomenon.

Although data on robbery trends in the United States are available only since the early 1930s, they display essentially the same pattern of change as homicide rates over this period. Robbery rates fell from over 100 robberies per 100,000 population in the early 1930s to about 50 per 100,000 population during the 1950s. They increased sharply during the 1960s to a level in recent years that is three to four times that observed during the 1950s. Even at their lowest point, however, U.S. robbery rates have far exceeded the highest rates observed in other societies.[22] Hence, although historical changes in rates of homicide and robbery in the United States are far from insignificant, and even allowing for considerable measurement error in the available statistics, it appears that the conditions contributing to the higher levels of these crimes in American society are related to *enduring* patterns of social organization that distinguish our society from other advanced industrial societies.

Race and Criminal Violence

A final factor that might explain why rates of serious crime are higher in the United States than in other industrial nations is ethnic heterogeneity. The United States is more ethnically and racially diverse than most other industrialized nations, and large differences in violent crime rates exist among racial and ethnic groups within American society. African Americans are overrepresented among both the victims and offenders in incidents of criminal violence. For example, blacks comprise 12 percent of the U.S. population but accounted for 50 percent of the nearly 24,000 homicide victims in 1992. The homicide victimization rate among black Americans is more than six times that of white Americans. Homicide is the second leading cause of death among American adolescents and young adults; it is the leading cause of death among young African Americans. Homicides contributed fully 52 percent of all the deaths in 1991 among black Americans fifteen to twenty-four years old. The proportion of deaths from homicide among whites of the same age was 12 percent. Based on levels of homicide victimization in the early 1990s, the lifetime probability of death caused by homicide for black males is 1 in 26, compared with 1 in 170 for white males, 1 in 125 for black females, and 1 in 503 for white females.[23]

We cannot think of a more alarming set of social indicators in the United States than these measures of risk for lethal violence among black Americans, especially young black males. However, as high as they are, levels of homicide victimization among black Americans do not explain fully the differences in homicide rates between the United States and other developed societies. At five homicides per 100,000 population, the rate of homicide victimization among whites, although well below the rate for blacks, is more than three times the average rate of homicide among the other nations compared in Figure 2–2. In a comparison of the 1986–87 homicide victimization rates of fifteen- to twenty-four-year-old males in twenty-two developed nations, two public health researchers found that the U.S. rate for white males was more than twice the rate in Scotland, the nation with the next highest level of homicide among young males. In only four U.S. states are homicide rates among young whites as low as the aggregate rates in the comparison countries.[24]

Given the overwhelmingly intraracial character of homicide (over 90 percent of all homicides involve victims and offenders of the same race), we may assume that these differences in homicide victimization reflect similar differences in offending between blacks and whites in the United States. This assumption is supported by available information on the racial characteristics of persons arrested for homicide. In contrast with most other offenses, the great majority of homicides are cleared by an arrest—an offender is picked up by the police and his or her race is recorded. The observed differences in the homicide arrest rates between blacks and whites do in fact correspond closely with racial differences in homicide victimization. Blacks are almost seven times as likely as whites to be arrested for homicide in the United States. Nonetheless, the white homicide arrest rate in 1992 of 4.8 per 100,000 population is higher than the homicide rates of the other developed nations shown in Figure 2–2. Racial differences notwithstanding, then, with respect to both offending and victimization, levels of lethal violence among white Americans are substantially greater than those for the total populations of other industrial nations.[25]

The importance of racial differences in crime within the United States, either as a theoretical issue for criminological inquiry or as a social problem with a particularly profound impact on racially disadvantaged groups, should not be minimized. (We discuss this issue in greater detail in Chapter 4.) Nor for that matter should we ignore the relationship between the extraordinary supply of weapons in private hands and the exceptionally high levels of interpersonal violence in America. The primary analytical focus of this book, however, is on variation in rates of crime at the level of nation-states, and a careful examination of the international statistics on violent crime suggests that the distinctiveness of the United States in comparison with other developed nations cannot be easily explained away by the greater availability of firearms or the disproportionate involvement in crime by minority groups. Moreover, some of the most serious acts of criminal offending rarely involve the use of guns and are committed by persons in positions of high status that typically are occupied by members of the dominant racial group. We now turn to these crimes committed by the well-to-do, the so-called "white-collar" crimes.

WHITE-COLLAR CRIMES

You are safer on the subway than in any country club in America, especially when it comes to the danger of corruption.

The best way to rob a bank is to own one.

As through this world I've rambled
I've seen lots of funny men.
Some rob you with a six gun
and some with a fountain pen.[26]

White-collar crimes, which generally are defined as crimes committed by persons against the organizations for which they work (embezzlement, for example) or on behalf of those organizations (for instance, price fixing), occur with great frequency in the United States and result in significant individual and collective harm. Unfortunately, reliable information is not available on differences across societies in the rates of white-collar offending. However, several studies have shown that white-collar criminality is common in American society. A pioneering study by Edwin Sutherland (1949), who coined the term *white-collar crime,* revealed a pattern of widespread illegality and repeat offending on the part of the seventy largest companies in the United States. Each of the corporations had at least one adverse decision against it by a regulatory agency or court over a twenty-year period, and the firms averaged fourteen adverse decisions. Nearly all of the corporations were "recidivists" in the sense of committing violations on a repeated basis.

The findings of Sutherland's research, conducted during the 1940s, have been confirmed in subsequent investigations of corporate offending. A 1980 study of nearly 600 major corporations found that 60 percent had a federal case brought against them over a two-year period; over 40 percent had two or more actions initiated against them. These figures reflect legal actions or adverse decisions against corporations and therefore understate by a substantial margin actual levels of corporate crime, much of which goes undetected. In the words of two corporate crime researchers, they represent only "the tip of the iceberg of total violations."[27]

White-collar offending is not only prevalent but also quite serious. The aggregate impact of white-collar offending is impossible to measure with any degree of precision, but scholars estimate that the costs of these crimes exceed those of conventional street crimes, which are themselves quite high. This applies both to the economic losses associated with offenses such as fraud, false advertising, and price fixing and to the injuries, disease, and deaths resulting from product safety violations, violations of workplace health and safety codes, and other "violent" white-collar offenses.[28]

A single white-collar crime, or a cluster of related offenses, can have a staggering monetary impact—or, from the offender's perspective, an immense financial return. For example, the cost to the public of the savings and loan crisis of the 1980s and 1990s is estimated at approximately $200 billion over the next decade and up to $500 billion by the year 2021. How much of this total derives directly from criminal activities, and how much results from interest rates, declines in the value of real estate, and other economic factors, are uncertain. What is clear, however, is that a weakened and unstable regulatory environment, created by the deregulation of the thrift industry in the early 1980s, fostered "a climate of criminal opportunity" that produced a financial catastrophe. In the unambiguous language of a journalist who covered the savings and loan scandal, "the lax attitude in Washington provided a gold mine for criminals."[29]

It is now generally accepted that white-collar crimes have an enormous economic impact on consumers and taxpayers. However, because their costs usually are calculated in the aggregate, the effects of white-collar crimes on individual victims are often obscured. Sometimes the direct consequences for individuals of white-collar offending are quite small, precisely because there are so many victims. A price-fixing scheme that generates millions of dollars in illegal profits to business owners may cost individual consumers only a few pennies more in higher prices. The impact of this kind of offense is more fully reflected in the number of victims rather than in the economic harm done to each one.

Yet it would be a mistake to minimize the individual impact of white-collar criminality. White-collar crimes can result in the loss of savings, homes, and jobs. Consider the case of a Wisconsin insurance and securities executive who was charged in the spring of 1992 with six counts of theft for keeping money he received for annuities investments. The executive, who fled Wisconsin when the charges were filed, was accused in one of the counts of taking $80,000 from an elderly couple and their children. In another, he was accused of stealing $20,000 from a ninety-year-old woman. Nearly all of his victims were elderly, and many were disabled.[30] Similarly tragic cases have been reported for telemarketing frauds. A recent FBI undercover operation in which volunteers tape-recorded dishonest telemarketers uncovered the case of an Ohio widow who lost $240,000 in life savings to such scams. Another incident involved a ninety-two-year-old California woman, who lost $180,000 to dishonest telemarketers.[31] Incidents like these underscore the very real economic harm that can be inflicted by white-collar offenders.

There should be no difficulty at all in appreciating the harmful consequences for individual victims of white-collar crimes that cause disease, injury, or death. However, clear and widely accepted standards for determining whether a white-collar crime is a "violent crime" do not exist. Most Americans would agree that an elderly woman who loses her savings in a fraudulent investment scheme is the victim of a crime. We seem to have more difficulty viewing the coal miner who develops black lung disease or the child who is injured while playing with an unsafe toy as crime victims. However, considerable evidence indicates that so-called "nonviolent" white-collar criminals kill and maim more people each year in the United States than do violent street criminals.

Each year, approximately 14,000 workers are killed on the job in the United States, and an additional 100,000 die from diseases related to their jobs. An estimated 140,000 people die every year from air pollution, and another 30,000 deaths result from unsafe or defective merchandise. Several million people are seriously injured by defective products or dangerous working conditions. Even if only one of every ten of these incidents were the result of criminal offenses or violations, they would still outnumber the yearly deaths and injuries from homicides and serious assaults in the United States.[32] In fact, 10 percent is a very conservative estimate of the deaths and injuries related to unsafe jobs, products, and environments that are attributable to white-collar crime. Studies have shown, for example, that as many as one-third to one-half of job-related accidents are the result of crimes or violations by employers.[33] When combined with the evidence on the economic impact of white-collar crime, findings such as these have prompted a leading analyst of white-collar crime to conclude that "by virtually any criterion…, white-collar crime is our most serious crime problem."[34]

SERIOUS CRIME AND THE QUALITY OF LIFE

The summary counts, rates, and comparative figures on crime and the costs of crime presented earlier are indispensable for describing, and ultimately explaining, the crime problem in the United States. However, the quantitative data alone do not capture adequately the social reality of serious crime.

Another, more qualitative dimension of experiences with crime is revealed in a different, but no less important or real, set of facts about the personal and social impacts of crime. We conclude this chapter, therefore, by supplementing the quantitative indicators of the crime problem with qualitative descriptions of the fear, anger, frustration, and desperation that form the texture of day-to-day living with serious crime.

Taking Precautions by Any Means Necessary

Although, as we noted in Chapter 1, the fear of crime is widespread in America, people take precautions against crime in all urban industrial societies. A 1988 cross-national survey found, for example, that between 20 and 40 percent of the populations of fourteen industrial nations were concerned enough about street crime to take one or more "precautionary measures" when out after dark. The United States ranked at the top of this comparison, but a number of other nations showed roughly comparable levels of crime avoidance.[35]

These survey data effectively describe what might be considered the normal level of fear characteristic of everyday life in most modern industrial societies. What the figures do not reveal, however, are the acute pockets of fear found in the high-crime neighborhoods of nearly all large American cities but in few other places in the industrialized world—except during wartime. Nor do the comparative statistics distinguish the standard protective measures undertaken by urban dwellers in all nations (such as avoiding certain streets or areas after dark) from the desperate and drastic responses described by the inhabitants of the "war zones" of urban America.

For example, a resident of a high-crime area in St. Louis described for a reporter the three "survival rules" that she and many of her neighbors live by: "Stay off the streets at night unless your life depends on it, keep your children indoors, and never sleep by a window." "We hit the floor," one of her neighbors recounted about a recent violent incident, when fourteen shots were fired into the house next to hers. "You do that a lot around here." One woman from the same neighborhood hides in her closet when the shooting begins. Another said she would buy a dog for protection were it not for her fear that the dog would be shot. Finally, an elderly woman from this area described the "little traps" for criminals she has set around her home, such as the bucket of water mixed with "something extra" balanced above one of the doors, the strands of "booby-trapped beads" that decorate another doorway, or the lawn mower set strategically at the top of a stairway. These contrivances, motivated by fear, were modeled after those created by a young boy to fend off burglars in the 1990 hit movie *Home Alone*. For this woman, the popular comedy was not a diversion from the rigors of everyday life but a recipe for dealing with them. She saw the film ten times.[36]

American men also tell "war stories" about the extraordinary, if not always effective, precautions they take against crime. A St. Louis man, who requires his children to sleep in a bedroom without windows, was preparing to take a bath one evening in the fall of 1992 when gunfire broke out near his house. "As soon as I heard the shooting, I jumped in the tub and lay down in the water," he told a reporter. "It didn't bother me at all that I still had my clothes on. I ruined a good watch." When he heard police sirens, the man ran to the scene of the shooting and found a woman he described as "a good friend" dying on the sidewalk in front of her home.[37] A seventy-eight-year-old man from a neighborhood nearby carried all of his money with him whenever he went out, fearing that it would be stolen if left unprotected in his house. He had good reason to be concerned. His home had been burglarized repeatedly, including once while he was in the hospital. On that occasion, all of his plumbing fixtures were taken. One early August morning, on the way to meet a friend for their regular breakfast at McDonald's, he was hit on the head and robbed of $300. He died from the wound a short time later. A woman who lived across the street from the victim was beaten up and stabbed. The victim's breakfast companion, meanwhile, had several of the windows in his home and in his car broken. He bought a rifle to add to the pistol he already owned for protection. He had used the pistol the previous week to run off some people who were trying to break down his front door. His protection plan was to fight fire with fire: "I'll tell you…, they ain't going to run me out. I can get as bad as they can get."[38] The odds do not appear to be in his favor. Even a courageous man with two guns can only hold out for so long against repeated attacks by forces beyond his control.

Life in a War Zone

It has become increasingly common to compare the terror and dangers of living in high-crime areas of America's major cities with those of living under conditions of warfare. A St. Louis woman compared her neighborhood to Bosnia's Sarajevo at the time of the intense ethnic conflict in that country during the early 1990s.[39] Similar comparisons were made between conditions in American cities and the tragic situation in Somalia when U.S. forces were deployed to provide security for agencies providing famine relief. For example, a *Newsweek* columnist asked:

> Why can the United States send forces halfway around the world to disarm Somali drug warlords but not halfway across town to disarm American drug warlords? Why is the government set up so that the national-security advisor each morning gives the President a briefing on world events…, but the war at home provokes little more than a few rhetorical expressions of sympathy?[40]

A resident of the South Bronx expressed sympathy for the starving Somalians but was angered by the contrast between the government's response to their plight and the reaction to his own: "It's right that they care and are trying to save lives, but I think that the United States has some gall. If they can't disarm the people in New York with guns, how are they going to go over someplace else and do it?"[41]

Nor are the comparisons of the dangers of American cities with those of war lost on those American soldiers who must survive in both contexts. A marine who thought he would find Somalia to be exotic and unfamiliar instead discovered conditions there distressingly like those in his neighborhood at home. "The fear of walking the streets without a gun, the fear of someone shooting at you, these are the things I go through every time I go back to D.C."[42]

As a final illustration of the parallels between the warlike conditions in major American cities and those of the battlefield, consider the case of Thanh Tan Le. Le was a former colonel in the South Vietnamese army who emigrated to the United States and was employed as a caseworker for the International Institute of Metropolitan St. Louis, an organization that assists immigrants from Vietnam and other countries in adjusting to the conditions of American life. While on his way to work one morning, he was fatally shot during a carjacking. The local news report on the killing pointed out that Le had survived his country's civil war and eight years in a reeducation camp in Vietnam, "but he couldn't survive the random street violence of American life."[43]

The Struggle for Institutional Control

Warlike conditions not only kill and maim individuals; they also destroy institutions. The relationship works in the opposite direction as well. When local institutions (for example, schools, businesses, families, police forces) are weakened, they lose their capacity to contain crime within manageable bounds. The escalating crime levels that result continue to assault ever more vulnerable institutions, in an ongoing spiral of "disorder and decline."[44]

Local institutions provide order, meaning, purpose, and protection to area residents. Much of the terror surrounding crime is due not simply to the threat of individual victimization but to the sense that the protective cover of institutions has collapsed, exposing individuals to all manner of unpredictable and uncontrollable dangers. In the spring of 1992, according to one news account, many residents of south central Los Angeles "were horrified during the riot at a lack of response from an overwhelmed Los Angeles Police Department." Even a gun shop owner was concerned for his safety when he saw the police retreat from looters: "The LAPD ran away in half a second," he told a reporter. "I never saw such a fast escape."[45]

However, in addition to institutions with formal responsibility for law enforcement, other institutions perform essential protective functions, often filling in for lapses or weaknesses in the functions of others. Consider the relationship between the family and the school. In all communities, schools supplement the family by providing essential socialization, support, and supervision for children. In some communities, the schools also offer a refuge from the dangers of the streets. A Chicago eleven-year-old wrote in a school essay on violence that he "can't go to school without rolling under cars and dodging bullets."[46] Once in school, however, the shooting is supposed to stop. A chilling illustration of the dependence of children on the protective function of schools in high-risk communities is the response of a student in St. Louis to a recent killing at her school: "I'm tired of it. You expect this to happen in your own backyard but not in your school."[47]

When the school is invaded by crime, therefore, children may feel doubly threatened: first by the crime itself, and second by the loss of one the few remaining safe havens left in the community. And the children may not be the only ones who are made fearful. A guidance counselor at a Chicago grade school explains, after a recent killing of a student:

> There have always been shootings before school and after school. But this happened right at school. It just became more real, more unbearable to everyone. Usually at times like this we just have to deal with the students and the parents. Now we have to deal with the teachers, too. It's just been too much.[48]

This process of institutional engulfment can eventually spread through entire communities, and it does so with disturbing frequency in urban areas across the United States. An example is the Englewood section of Chicago, which was transformed during the 1980s from a stable residential community into one of the most violent neighborhoods in the United States—and in the world.[49] Englewood's homicide rate of eighty-nine per 100,000 residents is nine times the rate for the United States as a whole. Ninety-six homicides occurred in Englewood during 1991, six more than the ninety homicides in all of Northern Ireland that year. The comparison is made all the more striking by the fact that Englewood's population of 108,000 is only one-fifteenth the size of Northern Ireland's.

The streets in Englewood are often empty during the day. Most children are not allowed to play outside after school. The remaining legitimate businesses in the area are secured with steel gates and rarely put their goods on display. By comparison, the drug trade flourishes, as do drug- and gang-related violence. The sounds of gunfire are unending. A sixty-three-year-old woman hears the shooting "every weekend, sometimes everyday and night." A teenager whose younger brother was recently killed by gang members worries that eventually he also will be shot: "They shoot around my house. They shoot everywhere you go."

Institutional engulfment and community decline often occur very rapidly, as in Englewood, but the process is not automatic, and it is intertwined with the personal struggles against crime described earlier. People do not willingly give up their homes, businesses, and communities. Many fight hard and make enormous sacrifices to protect their individual and institutional lives. A twenty-four-year-old college student quit school after the 1992 Los Angeles riot to help her aging parents run the family market in south central Los Angeles. She slept in the store for a month after the disorder. "In our family all we have is this store. This is our life. If we have no store, we don't eat."[50] Like other shop owners in the area, her family armed themselves in anticipation of further unrest. However, as destructive and terrifying as the riot was, it served only as a flash point in the family's ongoing struggle against crime and violence: "It's scary. They can kill you. It's scary all the time. They've robbed the store three times since last year. They put the gun up to my head." In response to such conditions, this young woman has, in the words of a reporter, "scaled back her

American dream." Her hope for the future is simply "to be where there is not so much danger."

Many Englewood residents have not given up in their struggle against crime. They organize antidrug rallies, form block associations, remain involved with the schools, attend church, and pray for the violence to stop. Yet they appear to be fighting a losing battle. The police report that little can be done to prevent the continuing spiral of violence. The only sure method of crime control may be the individual solution of moving to a safer area, "where there is not so much danger." Ironically, however, that is exactly the reason many of its current residents moved to Englewood, to escape even more blighted areas of the city.

As bad as conditions have become in Englewood, it remains an attractive alternative to other neighborhoods that are in even more advanced stages of decline. The utter institutional barrenness of such areas is reflected in a Chicago police officer's description of a once thriving community:

> Do you see any hardware stores? Do you see any grocery stores? Do you see any restaurants? Any bowling alleys? There is nothing here.... Nothing is worth anything in the area because you open up and you get knocked off, and you get knocked off, and you get knocked off until you give up.... In the last few months, three of the last gas stations closed up. The Church's Fried Chicken at Madison and Sacramento finally gave up after being robbed nine days in a row by nine different people.... You don't see any newspaper vending machines. Everything we take for granted—a laundromat, a cleaner's, anything. It's not here. The school dropout rate is 70 percent. What do these kids have to do? Nothing.[51]

How are these scenes of crime, institutional collapse, and community decline to be explained? If, as we have suggested, they are reminiscent of the personal struggles and social destruction of warfare, we must now probe the deeper issues suggested by this analogy. What makes living under conditions of serious crime in the United States so much like living under conditions of war? Why are local institutions so vulnerable to collapse? To answer these questions, we must look beyond the local battlegrounds of crime and violence and examine the broader cultural and social context in which local institutions function. The logical starting point for such inquiry is a review of the dominant theoretical perspectives on the cultural and social causes of crime.

NOTES

1. We found Barkley's joke about American crime on the sports page of a midwestern daily, buried in a wire story titled "Lithuania Is a Snap for U.S." (*St. Louis Post-Dispatch*, 1992a).

2. The 1991 Philadelphia crime figures were provided by personal communication with the Philadelphia Police Department.

3. Bureau of Justice Statistics (1992a, p. 8). Beginning in 1973, the NCVS has gathered information each year from a nationally representative sample of U.S. households about several types of household and personal crimes experienced by household members age twelve or older. For each victimization, respondents are

asked whether they reported the crime to the police. A full description of NCVS methods and data can be found in Bureau of Justice Statistics (1992a).

4. These calculations are based on Uniform Crime Reporting (UCR) data supplied by the St. Louis Metropolitan Police Department. Since the 1930s, the FBI's Uniform Crime Reporting Program has compiled crime statistics from information provided by local law enforcement agencies. The statistics are published annually in the volume *Crime in the United States*. Because the UCR crime figures are limited to offenses reported to and recorded by the police, they differ from the figures based on the victim surveys described earlier. Good discussions of this and other differences between the two crime data sources can be found in Biderman and Lynch (1991) and MacKenzie, Baunach, and Roberg (1990).

5. Gurr (1989, pp. 45–46). In addition to Gurr (1989), see Shelley (1981) for an overview of the modernization thesis on crime and of the historical research on long-term changes in the crime rates of industrial societies.

6. See LaFree and Kick (1986) and Neuman and Berger (1988) for comprehensive reviews of the cross-national research on crime and development.

7. See Archer and Gartner (1984) and Kalish (1988) for discussions of methodological problems associated with cross-national crime comparisons and useful approaches for addressing them.

8. The robbery data are from Interpol (1991–92). The most recent Interpol publication at the time of this writing contained figures for 1992 for most nations in Figure 2–1. The robbery data for Canada, Germany, and Australia are for 1991, 1990, and 1988, respectively. The homicide data for all nations other than the United States are from World Health Organization (1994), and the U.S. source is the U.S. Bureau of the Census (1995). Homicide rates for all nations refer to 1992, with the exception of Italy (1991). The definition of homicide presented in the text is reported in Kalish (1988, p. 4).

9. Sanger (1992).

10. *Johannesburg Star* (1996); *New York Times* (1996). The Russian homicide rate in 1992 was 22.9 per 100,000 population (World Health Organization, 1995).

11. See, for example, Lynch (1995, pp. 15–26); Mayhew (1993); Reichel (1994, pp. 28–46). Classification procedures for property crimes are likely to depress somewhat U.S. rates because of the "hierarchy rule." This rule results in only the most serious crime being recorded when multiple offenses are committed. For example, a carjacking is recorded as a robbery even though it also involves theft of a motor vehicle.

12. Bayley (1991, pp. 176–177).

13. See van Dijk, Mayhew, and Killias (1991, p. 94). With the exception of Japan and Denmark, each of the nations listed in Figures 2–1 and 2–2 was included in this survey.

14. Excellent reviews of research on the relationship between gun ownership and violent crime in the United States can be found in Kleck (1991) and Reiss and Roth (1993).

15. The data on gun-related homicides are from Federal Bureau of Investigation (1993b, p. 18, Table 2.8).

16. Kates (1989, p. 201).

17. Quotations and related material on this incident are from Sanger (1993). A subsequent killing of two Japanese students in Los Angeles during a carjacking aroused a similarly strong reaction among the Japanese public, leading the American ambassador to Japan, Walter Mondale, to go on national television to issue a public apology. See Sanger (1994).

18. Shelley (1981, p. 76).

19. Gurr (1989, p. 41).

20. The homicide data for 1900–1959 are based on medical examiners' records compiled in the *Vital Statistics* and reported in Archer and Gartner (1984). The data for 1960–1993 are based on UCR offense rates reported in Maguire and Pastore (1995, p. 305, Table 3.94). The series has been converted to a three-year moving average to reduce yearly fluctuations in the data. UCR data are unavailable before 1933. In spite of differences in the way

homicides are defined and measured in the *Vital Statistics* and UCR data, the two series display a nearly perfect correlation over the past fifty years or so (see Zahn, 1989, pp. 218–219).

21. Archer and Gartner (1984) report homicide time series of varying lengths for many of the nations compared in Figure 2–2.

22. See the robbery series for the United States, and several of the other nations displayed in Figure 2–1, in Archer and Gartner (1984).

23. The data on race differences in homicide victimization risk and homicide as a cause of death are from Federal Bureau of Investigation (1993b, p. 16, Table 2.4); U.S. Bureau of the Census (1994, p. 94, Table 126); and U.S. Public Health Service (1990, p. 16). The lifetime probabilities of death from homicide are reported in Dobrin et al. (1996, p. 285, Table 4.34).

24. The homicide victimization rate for whites was computed from 1992 homicide data reported in Federal Bureau of Investigation (1993b, p. 16, Table 2.4) and population data from U.S. Bureau of the Census (1994, p. 17, Table 17). The cross-national comparisons are reported in Fingerhut and Kleinman (1990).

25. Sharply lower arrest clearance rates and other data limitations preclude similar comparisons for robbery. Race-specific homicide arrest rates for 1992 are reported in Federal Bureau of Investigation (1993a, p. 173).

26. The first quote is from Keillor (1992); the second is from the testimony of the California savings and loan commissioner before a Congressional committee (U.S. Congress House Committee on Government Operations, 1988, p. 34). The third quote is from Woody Guthrie's song "Pretty Boy Floyd."

27. Sutherland's results are described in his book *White Collar Crime* (1949). The later study was conducted by Clinard and Yeager (1980), who characterize official actions against corporations as the "tip of the iceberg" of corporate crime (quoted in Kappeler, Blumberg, and Potter, 1993, p. 111).

28. A widely cited estimate of the annual monetary cost associated with corporate crime is the Senate Judiciary Subcommittee on Antitrust and Monopoly's figure of $174–$231 billion for the early 1970s (Kappeler et al., 1993, p. 104; Simon 1996, p. 269). Assuming no change in the real costs of corporate crime, and allowing only for inflation, the corresponding figure for the early 1990s would be $510–$677 billion. For further discussion of the costs of white-collar crime, see Coleman (1994, pp. 7–10). A recent report from the National Institute of Justice (Miller, Cohen, and Wiersema, 1996) estimates that "street crimes" generate $105 billion annually in "tangible" costs (property and productivity losses, and medical expenses). This figure increases to $450 billion annually when "intangible costs" such as "pain, emotional trauma, disability, and death risk" are included.

29. Calavita and Pontell (1991, p. 94); Robinson (1990, p. 293). The reference to a "climate of criminal opportunity" is from Hagan (1992, p. 14).

30. He was later found in Missouri and arrested on the Wisconsin charges (see Little, 1992).

31. *New York Times* (1995).

32. The figures on job-, product-, and environment-related deaths and injuries are from Kappeler et al. (1993, p. 104).

33. Kappeler et al. (1993, p. 105). For a recent illustration of a case in which failure to adhere to regulations issued by the Occupational Safety and Health Administration (OSHA) resulted in the death of two workers and the injury of three others, see Steyer (1995).

34. Coleman (1994, p. 10). For additional evidence on the extensiveness and seriousness of corporate and other forms of white-collar crime, see Ermann and Lundman (1982, 1987) and Farrell and Swigert (1985).

35. van Dijk et al. (1991, pp. 77–79).

36. These descriptions are from Hernon (1992).

37. Hernon (1992, p. 9A).

38. Bryan (1992).

39. Hernon (1992, p. 1A).

40. Alter (1992).

41. Richardson (1992). The *Newsweek* columnist quoted in the text, Jonathan Alter, expressed a similar concern in a later essay: "Why should we settle for peace in the Middle East without peace in the Middle West?" (Alter, 1993).

42. *Newsweek* (1992).

43. Bryan (1996).

44. See Skogan (1990) for an extended discussion of these processes.

45. Mydans (1993, p. 12).

46. Quoted in Terry (1992, p. 6).

47. Quoted in Bryan and Little (1993, p. 1A). A rather extreme approach to protecting minority children from such violence has been proposed in a *New York Times* editorial. The columnist draws an analogy between the situation in contemporary American cities and that in London during the blitzkrieg when Britons sent their children out of the city: "What American cities need are evacuation plans to spirit at least some black boys out of harm's way before its too late" (Staples, 1993).

48. Terry (1992). For an account of a teacher's effort to protect a student from an armed attack by a gang in a St. Louis classroom, see Little (1994).

49. This description of Englewood during the early 1990s is from the *Chicago Tribune* (1991).

50. This and the following quoted material is from Mydans (1993, p. 12).

51. Quoted in Soll (1993, p. 57).

3

Ships in the Night: Theoretical Perspectives in Contemporary Criminology

Ships that pass in the night, and speak each other in passing,
Only a signal shown and a distant voice in the darkness;

So on the ocean of life, we pass and speak one another,
Only a look and a voice, then darkness again and a silence.

HENRY WADSWORTH LONGFELLOW
"THE THEOLOGIAN'S TALE: ELIZABETH"

James F. Short, Jr., past president of both the American Society of Criminology and the American Sociological Association, has called attention to a problem that is pervasive in scholarly debates as well as in everyday discourse. Very often spirited exchanges seem to go nowhere because the participants fail to recognize that they are not really talking about the same thing. Like ships that pass in the night, the verbal combatants talk past one another.[1] Not surprisingly, such debates are likely to generate more heat than light on the topic under consideration.

In this chapter, we try to forestall this kind of miscommunication—first, by clearly delimiting the *scope conditions* of our explanation of the American crime problem and, second, by making explicit the set of concepts and assumptions underlying our approach, that is, by making explicit our analytic paradigm.[2] The scope conditions of an explanation specify the limits within which its claims are assumed to hold. Our explanation of the American crime problem has two key scope conditions. One concerns the *level* of explanation, and the other involves the seriousness of the crimes to which the explanation applies.

As the evidence presented in the previous chapter suggests, we seek to explain *macrolevel* differences (that is, differences across groups or populations) in rates of the most serious types of crime. Our analysis is not directly concerned with the *individual-level* question of why some persons are more or less likely than others to commit criminal acts. Nor does our explanation encompass the types of crimes that are generally regarded by the public, policy makers, and criminologists alike as less serious than the forms of criminal violence and very serious economic crimes addressed in Chapter 2.

By contrast, the major theoretical perspectives on crime and delinquency are oriented to the individual level of analysis and, while not precluding serious crimes, have tended to focus on less serious forms of offending. Their scope conditions, in other words, are exactly the opposite of those guiding our explanation of crime. Theories with different scope conditions cannot be compared directly because they seek to explain different phenomena. It is possible, however, to link these individual-level theories of crime with macrolevel explanations that share a similar causal logic. These macrolevel explanations can then be evaluated in terms of their ability to explain variation in the rates of serious crimes.

In the second part of this chapter, we introduce the sociological paradigm informing our analysis and argue that the failure of major theoretical perspectives within contemporary criminology to offer a satisfactory explanation of macrolevel variation in crimes results from either a distorted or underdeveloped use of this analytical framework. Our review encompasses the major individual-level perspectives in criminology—social learning, control, and strain—and their macrolevel analogues—cultural deviance, social disorganization, and anomie. Among the existing perspectives, anomie theory comes closest, in our view, to providing a compelling account of the American crime problem. However, anomie theory also requires considerable clarification and expansion to fully realize its explanatory potential. In Chapter 4, we present a sociological explanation of crime based on a revised version of anomie theory that is capable of accounting for the comparatively high rates of serious crime in the United States.

THE SCOPE CONDITIONS OF CONTEMPORARY CRIMINOLOGICAL THEORIES

Levels of Explanation

One of the primary reasons for miscommunication in debates about crime is confusion over levels of explanation.[3] Much of the inquiry into crime, by professional criminologists and laypersons alike, occurs at the *individual* level of analysis. The basic question underlying the individualistic approach, as noted earlier, is why one person rather than another commits a criminal act. The answer to this type of question is properly cast in terms of attributes or predispositions of individuals, including biological traits, psychological states, and personal socialization experiences.

In contrast, analysis at the *macrolevel* focuses on questions about groups and populations. The relevant questions here include the following: Why do levels of crime vary across social systems (for example, nations, cities, neighborhoods)? Why is crime patterned in systematic ways across social categories within a social system (for instance, by race, class, age, gender)? Macrolevel questions are framed in terms of rates of crime. Crime rates are constructed by adding up all of the individual acts of crime recorded in a particular area or ostensibly committed by (or against) members of a specified group or category. In practice, the construction of crime rates is a complex process reflecting the decisions and behaviors of those reporting victimizations and those recording these incidents. Crime rates ultimately reflect not merely the level of some kind of behavior but the "criminalization" of that behavior as well.[4] Nevertheless, the rate itself does not really describe any given individual. Rather, the crime rate is a property of a human aggregate. Émile Durkheim referred to such properties as *social facts* and argued convincingly that social facts are best explained by other social facts. In other words, questions about crime rates, unlike questions about individual acts of crime, are most appropriately explained with reference to other properties of collective units.[5]

The distinction between individual- and macrolevel explanations is important because neither can be fully reduced to the other. To illustrate, consider the phenomenon of unemployment. A plausible explanation for why one person rather than another loses his or her job might be formulated in terms of education. Evidence indicates that the risk of unemployment decreases along with the attainment of higher levels of education. In the 1993 General Social Survey, for example, respondents with a college education were only half as likely as those with just a high school degree to be unemployed. High school graduates, in turn, were substantially less likely to be out of work than respondents who had not completed high school. This relationship between education and unemployment at the individual level is shown in the bar graph embedded in Figure 3–1.

The relationship between individual educational attainment and unemployment risk, however, is not reflected in the relationship between aggregate educational characteristics of the U.S. population and the rate of unemployment. The relative size of the college-educated population has climbed steadily over recent decades, increasing from 7.7 percent in 1960, to 10.7 percent in 1970, 16.2 percent in 1980, and 21.9 percent in 1993. On the basis of the individual-level relationship between education and unemployment, then, one might expect that the nation's unemployment rate would decline as a result of the substantial growth of the college educated population during this period. Yet unemployment rates have not fallen, adjusting for cyclical fluctuations. If anything, as shown in Figure 3–1, the overall trend in levels of unemployment over recent decades has been slightly upward.[6]

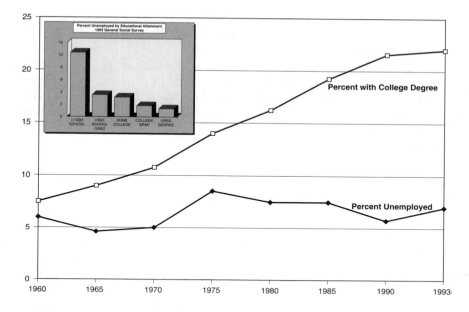

FIGURE 3–1 Two Views of the Education-Unemployment Relationship

Note also that "macroeconomic" explanations for the rate of unemployment are often formulated using concepts that are not directly applicable to individual-level analysis because they do not describe properties of persons. The precise causes of unemployment levels are not fully understood, but many economists point to factors such as interest rates, governmental transfer programs (unemployment insurance, food stamps), tax policies, and international trade deficits. No strict counterparts exist at the individual level for these macrolevel concepts. As a result, explanations of unemployment rates that employ such concepts will necessarily differ from individual-level explanations.

An example of criminological research that explicitly recognizes the distinction between levels of explanation is Hodgins's study of the impact of mental disorder and intellectual deficiency on criminal behavior in a Swedish birth cohort. The study found that persons with mental disorders and intellectual deficits were significantly more likely than others to commit both property and violent crimes. However, Hodgins cautions against generalizing these individual-level findings to the macrolevel. For example, the results cannot account for differences in crime rates between the United States and Sweden, because levels of mental disorder and intellectual deficiency are about the same in the two nations. Moreover, given the high rates of crime in the United States, "the crimes of those with major psychiatric disorders and intellectual handicaps seem insignificant in comparison."[7]

We do not mean to suggest that individual-level inquiry is unimportant; it obviously is indispensable for a comprehensive understanding of crime. Any macrolevel explanation of crime will inevitably be predicated on underlying premises about individual behavior.[8] We simply want to emphasize that our objectives in this book are distinctly macrolevel in character. Indeed, it is precisely because the questions that we ask are questions about aggregate patterns of crime that we employ an explanatory framework built around basic properties of social organization. We rely on one set of social facts—features of social organization such as culture and social structure—to explain another set of social facts—American crime rates compared with those of other developed nations.

Serious Crimes

In addition to limiting our focus to macrolevel questions, we also restrict the scope of the analysis to a specific domain of criminal behavior, namely, serious crimes. By this we mean violations of criminal law involving significant bodily injury, the threat of bodily injury, or, in the case of nonviolent offenses, significant economic harm to victims, both individual and collective. What distinguishes significant from nonsignificant threats and harms is inherently arbitrary. Consequently, it is best to think of crimes as arrayed on a continuum, from the most serious at one end to the least serious at the other.[9] The evidence and arguments that we present are, with few exceptions, restricted in application and scope to the serious end of the continuum.

It might seem self-evident that criminologists should devote most of their attention to crimes that nearly everyone regards as serious. However, modern criminology is not, by and large, devoted to the study of serious offending. On the contrary, research carried out to test the leading perspectives in the field tends to be dominated by studies of "relatively trivial offenses," a characterization that has been applied specifically to empirical research associated with the control theory of crime and delinquency.[10] Control theory, which emphasizes individual restraints against the temptations of crime, is arguably the dominant theoretical perspective within criminology today. A survey of articles published between 1964 and 1992 in *Criminology*, the official journal of the American Society of Criminology, found that the control perspective is "by far" the most frequently tested theory in the discipline. Studies of crime generated by other criminological perspectives also tend to focus on comparatively minor illegalities.[11]

The neglect of serious offending by contemporary criminologists is not explained by professional disagreements over what types of crime are most serious. Few criminologists would dispute the claim that homicide and robbery, for example, are serious crimes. Part of the reason that criminologists have not paid more attention to such offenses is methodological. Because serious offending is engaged in by small numbers of people, it is difficult to study via the survey research methods that have been favored by recent generations of researchers. Prohibitively large samples would have to be drawn from the general population to secure a sufficient number of street criminals or corporate criminals for reliable analysis, even assuming such persons would tell the truth about their illegal activities. Yet there are other ways of obtaining information from people who commit serious crimes (for example, they can be interviewed in prison), and, ideally, the choice of research issues should not be driven by methodological considerations.[12]

Another possible reason for the relative neglect of serious crimes in contemporary criminology is more substantive in nature. It might be argued that serious crimes do not warrant extensive attention precisely because they are so infrequent. In other words, because many fewer people are affected by serious crimes than by nonserious crimes, the aggregate (if not individual) harm associated with serious crimes might be regarded as less than that of nonserious crimes, thereby rendering the former less important for analytical purposes. The problem with this line of reasoning is that it understates the frequency and impact of serious offending, especially in the category of white-collar crime. In addition, a full appreciation of the practical importance of serious crimes requires an assessment of both their frequency relative to less serious crimes and their frequency relative to other behaviors or conditions that result in significant harm (such as automobile accidents and infectious disease). A fundamental reason that interpersonal violence is now recognized as a public health problem as well as a law enforcement problem in the United States is because, in the words of two public health researchers, it "exacts such a high toll in illness, death and quality of life."[13]

Homicide is the tenth leading cause of death in the United States and the third leading cause of premature mortality from injury, after motor vehicle accidents and suicide. Over a quarter of the 10,000 to 15,000 spinal cord injuries that occur each year in the United States result from violent assaults. In Detroit, 40 percent of the traumatic spinal cord injuries result from gunshot wounds. Criminal violence takes a particularly tragic toll on the young and African Americans. Homicide is the third leading cause of death (after accidents and suicides) among white teenagers and young adults, and, as reported in Chapter 2, it is the leading cause of death among black teenagers and young adults. Even acknowledging that these comparisons reflect declines in other causes of injury and death as well as increased risk from criminal violence, it can hardly be said that serious crime is a rare cause of death or physical injury in the United States.[14]

Finally, it has been argued that, regardless of their frequency or effects, serious crimes do not require special explanation; they can be explained by the same perspectives that are applied to less serious crimes. Two criminologists have recently presented a "general" theory of crime (that is, a theory with very broad scope conditions) that does not distinguish between more serious and less serious forms of criminality.[15] The empirical foundation for our analysis, however, is the evidence of comparatively high levels of serious crime in the United States, as reported in the previous chapter. We are uncertain as to whether the United States would exhibit distinctively high levels of offending for minor offenses. In fact, it seems plausible that relatively minor legal violations are commonplace throughout the modern world and that appreciable differences among nations are likely to emerge only for criminal behaviors closer to the serious pole of the crime continuum. We thus prefer to leave open the possibility that explanations of serious crimes may differ in important respects from explanations of other crimes, and we restrict the scope conditions of our arguments accordingly.

The explanation of crime that we offer differs, then, in important respects from those that currently dominate criminological thinking. At the same time, however, our analysis of the American crime problem draws heavily from existing perspectives. We do not reject contemporary explanations of crime; rather, we seek to recast them in a broad macrosociological conceptual framework capable of accounting for variations across societies in rates of serious crime.

THE UNFULFILLED PROMISE OF THE SOCIOLOGICAL PARADIGM

A basic axiom of sociological analysis is that human behavior can be understood as a product of social organization. The two basic dimensions of social organization are culture and social structure. In sociological usage, *culture* refers to values, beliefs, goals, and norms—the entire "symbolic-meaningful" level of human action. *Social structure* consists of the patterned relationships among persons and groups defined and organized through social institutions.[16] The basic concepts of culture and social structure, and assumptions about their interrelationships, give rise to the sociological paradigm. In this book, we apply the general sociological paradigm to the specific social phenomenon of crime.

The major theoretical perspectives in contemporary criminology usually are described as sociological, but they are in fact more accurately viewed as social psychological in orientation. *Social learning theory,* for example, emphasizes the ways in which individuals acquire beliefs, attitudes, and behavior patterns conducive to crime. *Social control theory* posits that criminal behavior results when the individual's bonds to others are weakened. *Strain theory* proposes that criminality results from negative experiences, especially goal frustration associated with the discrepancy between an individual's aspirations, on the one hand, and achievements or expectations, on the other.

Although these perspectives have been formulated in individualistic terms, they can be related to companion macrolevel theories, which have a more distinctly sociological cast. Social learning theories are associated with what have been termed *cultural deviance theories,* which explain crime as the product of cultural or subcultural values and norms. Social control theory is most closely connected with *social disorganization theory* at the macrolevel of analysis. *Social disorganization* refers to the inability of groups or communities to realize collective goals, including the goal of crime control. Finally, strain theory is commonly linked with *anomie theory.* In its most general formulation, *anomie* refers to a weakening in the normative regulation of behavior. Anomie theory posits that social norms begin to lose their regulatory force when people are unable to realize their cultural goals by using the institutionally approved means.

The macrolevel criminological perspectives are most directly relevant to our analysis because they share the same scope conditions. However, the explanations of crime associated with these perspectives commonly contain references to individual behavior. In this sense, the macrolevel perspectives themselves are not consistently or exclusively sociological. It is most useful, then, to think of dominant criminological approaches as "hybrid" theories—cultural-social learning, disorganization-control, and anomie-strain—that actually combine individual- and macrolevel concepts and empirical referents.

The relationship between macrolevel theory and individual-level processes is actually quite complex and the subject of considerable debate among criminologists. For example, although the anomie perspective is most commonly linked with strain theory at the individual level, several criminologists have argued that a "control" model of individual behavior is also compatible with the logic of anomie theory.[17] We follow the conventional practice of joining strain and anomie theory in our review of existing criminological theories. As will become clear in Chapter 4, our proposed macrolevel explanation of crime incorporates elements from each of the three major "hybrid" perspectives on crime.

In addition to the cultural-social learning, disorganization-control, and anomie-strain perspectives, two other major theoretical perspectives are often considered sociological: the labeling (or "societal reaction") perspective and the conflict perspective. The principal contribution of *labeling theory* is to call attention to the interplay between social control and personal identity. Labeling theorists specify the processes through which efforts at crime control contribute to the stabilization of criminal roles and self-images. *Conflict theories* emphasize the political nature of crime production, posing the question of how the norms of particular groups are encoded into law and how, in turn, law is used as a means of domination of certain groups by others.

Both of these perspectives contain important insights about the creation and enforcement of rules in a society, but neither perspective focuses primarily on the causes of the behavior that is subject to labeling or criminalization by political authorities. Our inquiry is oriented toward questions about the causes of variation in rates of criminal behavior, and accordingly we focus our attention on those theoretical perspectives that address such questions directly: the "etiological" perspectives on crime.[18]

In the discussion that follows, we seek to place the major etiological perspectives within a broad sociological framework. Each of the perspectives is associated with a dimension of social organization. *Cultural-learning* explanations emphasize how crime varies with the strength of criminal subcultures. *Disorganization-control* explanations emphasize the structural dimension, specifically, how crime rates vary with the strength of social relationships and social controls. Finally, *anomie-strain* theory unites the two dimensions of social organization in its explanation of crime. Although each perspective offers a unique contribution to an explanation of crime at the macrolevel, each is also limited in important respects. Our analysis is intended to build on the strengths of the alternative perspectives and, at the same time, to overcome their limitations by joining them in a single, unifying paradigm.

Cultural-Learning Explanations of Crime

"A person becomes delinquent," Edwin Sutherland writes, "because of an excess of definitions favorable to violation of law over definitions unfavorable to violation of law."[19] Sutherland's principle of differential association lies at the center of cultural and subcultural explanations of crime. Criminal behavior is learned behavior, Sutherland insists, and it is learned under the same conditions and in the same ways conforming behavior is learned—in association with like-minded others. Social reinforcement and cultural validation are required whether one is learning to become a butcher or a dentist, a burglar or a rapist.

A source of the tremendous appeal and genuine importance of Sutherland's formulation is this normalizing focus. Criminal behavior is normal in the sense that it requires socially learned motivations and socially structured supports. Crime is normal, in a word, because it is social, and it is no less social than conformity.

However, Sutherland's idea and, by implication, all cultural explanations of crime go further. Crime not only arises from the same social sources as conformity; crime *is* conformity. Cultural explanations of deviance assume that people violate the normative standards of groups to which they do not belong by conforming to the standards of the groups to which they do belong. The famous example, introduced into the literature by Thorsten Sellin, is the Sicilian father who expresses surprise at his arrest by New Jersey authorities for killing the seducer of his teenage daughter. He was, after all, only doing what he had to do to uphold the conduct codes of "the old country."[20]

The general proposition that may be derived from accounts such as this one is as follows: Deviation from the standards of group or subgroup A is caused by conformity to the standards of group or subgroup B. People violate the standards of groups to which they do not belong. As a corollary, they do not, at least not in the theoretically interesting case, violate the standards of the groups to which they do belong. Critics have responded to these propositions from cultural deviance theory by arguing, reasonably enough, that the theory has no answer to the question of why someone might violate his or her own rules.[21]

Actually, the theory does have an answer for this question; however, it is an answer that supports the critics' general point. The answer is found in the idea of *culture conflict*. In all societies, people belong to many social groups, not just one. In highly complex urban industrial societies, in particular, these multiple group memberships may expose people to conflicting behavioral standards. To conform to one is, ipso facto, to violate another. This idea of crime as produced by culture conflict still remains rooted in a theory of crime-as-conformity. In culture-conflict explanations, just as in cultural explanations of crime more generally, deviance remains but the residual consequence of conformity. Without conformity, there is no (cultural) deviance.

In an important sense, then, cultural "deviance" theories are not theories of deviance at all. This is their distinctive strength, and it is their major shortcoming as an explanation of crime and other forms of deviance. To reiterate, the strength of the cultural-social learning perspective is that it calls attention to the normal character of much deviant behavior. It provides a purely social (or social-psychological) explanation of behavior and does not rely on or imply underlying psychological abnormality. It highlights the irony of deviance by showing how the extraordinary results from the ordinary, how the very conspiracy of the normal—the intensity and effectiveness of a group's efforts to promote conformity to its norms—produces the abnormal. The explanation of crime that we develop in this book is heavily indebted to this insight.

However, the idea that criminal behavior is learned (at the individual level) and that crime is entirely the product of culture (at the macrolevel) quickly runs into several interrelated problems. The perspective risks the danger of circular reasoning. If one assumes that all behavior is consistent with underlying values, then criminal acts themselves must be regarded as evidence of the presence of criminal values. The theory then becomes nonfalsifiable: Criminal acts will always be associated with criminal values. Any effort to restrict the scope conditions of the perspective to only certain kinds of crime ultimately leads to the same problem. Cultural theories, then, explain those crimes for which there is cultural support; in other words, the theory explains those crimes that it is capable of explaining!

Circular reasoning is also encouraged by the adoption of an overly broad conception of culture. Ruth Kornhauser identifies the omnibus definition of culture as the central analytical deficiency in the cultural approach to deviance. She writes:

> When everything is included under the rubric of culture, nothing is left with which to compare the causal importance of culture. How can such theories be tested? If culture includes all learned behavior irrespective of whether it is directed toward the realization of cultural values, then culture will always be the sole cause of behavior. If culture includes social organization, then the constraints imposed by the patterning of social relationships will simply be viewed as culturally determined.[22]

Finally, the cultural perspective runs the risk of trivialization. There is something inherently unsatisfying about an explanation of crime that simply describes cultural differences between criminals and noncriminals. Ernest van den Haag has summarized the problem concisely: "Surely crime is largely produced by the life styles generated by the subcultures characteristic of those who commit it. But does this tell us more than that crime is produced by a crime-producing subculture?"[23]

What produces the crime-producing subculture? Where do "definitions favorable to law violation" or "reinforcements for deviant behavior" come from? If criminal behavior is the product of socialization into the conduct codes of deviant subcultures, then to avoid trivialization and circularity, the cultural explanation of crime must account for the emergence, prevalence, content, and strength of deviant subcultures. This is difficult to do without recourse to the other dimension of social organization—social structure.[24]

Disorganization-Control Explanations of Crime

Disorganization-control explanations focus precisely on the structural dimension of social organization. Theorists in this camp maintain that criminality is the consequence not of culture but of the absence of culture. From the disorganization-control perspective, there is no need to account for a culturally induced "motivation" to break the rules. Driven by strong biological urges and pure self-interest, human beings are naturally predisposed to deviate. The basic question posed by control theory is not why some people break the rules but, rather, why the rest of us do not.[25]

The answer to this question is that most people obey the rules because they are restrained by social controls. Those who become criminal are thus those who lack such controls. Or, in Travis Hirschi's more elaborate formulation, people deviate from conventional rules of conduct because the bonds that attach them to others, commit them to conventional lines of action, involve them in conventional activities, and sustain their belief in the cultural standards themselves weaken or break.

Control theory is often faulted for begging the question of why bonds weaken or fail to develop in the first place. However, its macrolevel analogue—social disorganization theory—offers a partial answer to this question. Social disorganization theory was developed by sociologists at the University of Chicago in the early twentieth century. The work of the Chicago School sociologists has inspired a tradition of inquiry into the social ecological organization of the city. The resulting orientation to the spatial patterning of behavior in urban areas has given rise, in turn, to what has been aptly termed "neighborhood criminology."

The classic neighborhood criminologists were Clifford R. Shaw and Henry D. McKay, who applied the basic principles of the Chicago School to explain neighborhood crime rates.[26] Neighborhoods with the highest crime rates are those, Shaw and McKay argued, with high levels of residential instability, ethnic heterogeneity, and, most important, economic deprivation. These conditions erode the capacity of local institutions—businesses, schools, churches, families—to impose controls over the behavior of residents, especially children and adolescents. Moreover, weakened neighborhoods are unable to withstand or control "invasions" of new residents, who may bring with them distinct cultural traditions that impede communication and cooperation with older inhabitants. Even in the absence of cultural differences, the continuous arrival of new people (and the departure of former inhabitants) makes it difficult to maintain the kin and friendship networks, and the more formal associations, necessary for effective crime control. Shaw and McKay used the term *social disorganization* to describe the inability of a neighborhood to manage its boundaries, ward off invasion, and prevent delinquency and crime—in short, to "control itself." Their theory of social disorganization and neighborhood social control has undergone important changes over the last half century or so. Yet the basic idea that crime rates vary with a community's capacity to control the behavior of its members remains intact.[27]

The essential contribution of the control-disorganization perspective to a sociological explanation of crime is that it can answer the question that is not addressed adequately by learning and cultural deviance theory, namely, why people violate rules of the groups to which they belong. Moreover, control and social disorganization theorists justly criticize cultural deviance theorists for overemphasizing cultural support for crime and underemphasizing the lack of structural support for conformity. Yet, in spite of the fact that they are conceptual opposites, or perhaps because of it, control-disorganization theorists end up committing the same type of analytical error committed by cultural-learning theorists: they expunge from the explanatory framework one of the two fundamental features of social organization, in this case, culture.

Disorganization-control theorists and researchers have gone to great lengths in recent years to expel culture from the causes of crime. The crusade against culture stems in part from the understandable desire to avoid association with the "pathological" tradition in the study of American social problems, which tended to equate disorganization with deviation from small-town, Protestant, middle-class standards.[28] Also, as pointed out earlier, there are very real problems associated with the "pure" cultural explanations of crime and deviance, such as the overly broad conception of culture. Yet the response of control-disorganization theorists has been to propose an equally broad conception of "structure."

An apt illustration is provided in the work of Ruth Kornhauser, whose criticisms of the cultural approach have already been noted. As a corrective to an overly expansive concept of culture, Kornhauser proposes restricting the realm of culture to the "ultimate" ends and meanings of existence. Not all values, she insists, are cultural values, and not all symbolic meanings are located in culture. Cultural values specify the end points, not the instrumental means, of human action; cultural symbols are those, and only those, "richly elaborated in their meaning for the self."[29]

Kornhauser's restrictive definition of culture makes cultural explanation of any kind nearly impossible. How much social behavior, conforming or deviant, that occurs with any frequency is, after all, directly anchored to the end points of existence? The difficulty with her conception of culture is a mirror image of the conceptual problem she so deftly analyzes in cultural deviance theory. If cultural theorists amplify culture, packing it so full of meaning that it loses any distinctive analytical usefulness, then Kornhauser similarly distorts the concept of social structure. It must be asked, if not all values are cultural values—indeed, if most are not—then what else could they be? Kornhauser's answer is the only one possible: They are "structural values."[30]

Kornhauser's notion of structural values has two fundamental problems. First, her expansive view of structure makes it virtually impossible in practice to assess the importance of structural factors relative to cultural ones. This is exactly analogous to the problem associated with cultural theories recognized by Kornhauser herself. Hardly anything is "left out" of structure with which structural variables could be compared.

Second, the concept of structural values, if taken literally, undermines the essential distinction between the two components of social organization. The meanings of *culture* and *social structure* must be kept unambiguously distinct precisely because they are empirically inseparable. Culture and social structure are not "things" that can be neatly separated. They are analytical constructs that call attention to different aspects of the same underlying social phenomena. They are different ways of perceiving and understanding the nature of social reality and the causes of social behavior. They are, in brief, points of view for analyzing the social world.

Kornhauser acknowledges the importance of making an analytical distinction between the two dimensions of social organization. She applauds a classic statement by Kroeber and Parsons that sought to end, or at least to clarify, the dispute between anthropologists and sociologists concerning the relative significance of culture and social structure.[31] Yet her treatment of social organization runs counter to their instruction. For Kroeber and Parsons, there could be no such thing as a "structural value." Their point in setting forth an explicit distinction between the two dimensions of social organization was to prevent this kind of absorption of one by the other. *Social structure* should be limited in scope to the "relational" or interactional component of social systems. *Culture* should be limited to the dimension of value, belief, and knowledge. To blur this distinction, in their view and ours, destroys the analytical usefulness of both concepts.

The Common Origins of Cultural Deviance Theory and Social Disorganization Theory

Remembering that the concepts of culture and social structure, like all concepts, are analytical tools helps make sense of an otherwise very puzzling aspect of the history of sociological studies of crime in America. Both cultural deviance theory and its putative rival, social disorganization theory, were developed at essentially the same time, in the same place, by many of the same people, and in response to the same social reality: the early twentieth-century urban slum.

The connection between the preeminent cultural theory, Sutherland's theory of differential association, and Shaw and McKay's theory of social disorganization is particularly noteworthy. Differential association theory was originally conceived within a broader conceptual framework that attributed crime to both cultural conflict and structural disorganization. In an early formulation of his theory, Sutherland notes that what he termed "systematic" (that is, patterned and continuous) criminal behavior "is due immediately to differential association in a situation in which cultural conflicts exist, and ultimately to the social disorganization in that situation."[32]

After World War II, Sutherland broke with the social disorganization tradition in the sociology of crime. He explicitly rejected the very idea of social disorganization in favor of the concept of *differential social organization*. According to this view, crime rates tend to be higher in poor urban areas not because these areas lack social order but because they are apt to contain multiple sub-cultures, some of which are organized around "definitions favorable to law violation." The subgroups that carry such definitions are no less "organized" for promoting criminal rather than conforming behavior.[33]

Sutherland's break with disorganization theory did not occur because the urban social world that he observed differed from the one observed by the disorganization theorists. Again, the difference between the cultural deviance and social disorganization perspectives is more conceptual than empirical. The difference is fundamentally a matter of which elements of social reality an observer chooses to "see" and considers theoretically important. Because all groups of any complexity will contain some normative patterns that conflict with the law and some social structures that are too weak to sustain conformity to law, it is not surprising that social disorganization theorists could identify the degree of disorganization in a group as a relevant factor for explaining crime, while cultural theorists could focus on group (or subgroup) support for crime.

We know that the differences between cultural deviance and social disorganization researchers that originally emerged within the Chicago School are not primarily due to differences in the empirical phenomena that they observed, because both sides claim the same observers—Shaw and McKay—as in their own camp. And both sides are correct. Shaw and McKay held that social disorganization in an urban area produces delinquency, directly by weakening community controls, and indirectly by generating a subculture of delinquent "traditions" that is passed on over time by one generation of delinquents to another. Once it emerges, the delinquent subculture attains a life of its own, and it in fact becomes part of the organization of some lower-class communities. Shaw and McKay's explanation of crime is based, therefore, on a mixed model of community social organization, combining key elements of both social disorganization theory (for example, weak ties to conventional institutions) and cultural deviance theory (for instance, socialization into delinquent codes).[34]

Explanations of crime based on mixed models are not universally popular in contemporary criminology. Control theorists have a particularly strong disdain for them.[35] For example, Kornhauser describes Shaw and McKay's disorganization-subcultural explanation of delinquency as "untenable," maintaining that it produced a "confusion between cause and effect that plagues delinquency theory to this day." She concludes that Shaw and McKay's model is not only mixed but contradictory: its social disorganization assumptions cannot be true if its cultural deviance assumptions are also true.[36] Even if Kornhauser's assessment of Shaw and McKay's explanation is correct, however, it would not necessarily invalidate other explanations of crime based on such mixed models.

In any case, our point in reviewing the common theoretical origins of cultural theory and disorganization theory is to suggest that any explanation of crime that fully exploits the sociological paradigm will be, to one degree or another, a mixed-model explanation. This is because the sociological paradigm is itself a mixed model. It relates crime to social organization, which encompasses both culture and social structure. Far from viewing this as a shortcoming, we think that criminological explanation can only benefit from an analytical framework that calls attention to both aspects of social reality. The third major perspective in criminology—anomie-strain theory—has the virtue of applying the sociological paradigm in its totality rather than in the fractured form characteristic of other contemporary approaches.

Anomie-Strain Explanations of Crime

Anomie theory is capable of answering the questions about the causes of crime left open or defined away by the cultural learning and disorganization perspectives. These perspectives are deficient, we have argued, because they exaggerate the causal importance of one of the dimensions of social organization—structure in the case of disorganization theory and culture in the case of cultural theory—and downplay the importance of the other dimension. By contrast, anomie theory incorporates both dimensions in an explanation that, whatever its *empirical* failings, has the great advantage of being *conceptually* complete.

Robert Merton presented the classic formulation of anomie theory in his 1938 essay "Social Structure and Anomie." He clarified and expanded, but did not fundamentally alter, his thesis in papers published over the succeeding several decades.[37] When cast in the terms of the sociological paradigm described earlier, Merton's theory attributes crime to the lack of articulation within and between the basic components of social organization: culture and social structure. Merton subdivides culture (what he refers to as the "culture structure") into two parts: (1) the society's central value and goal orientations, or *ends,* and (2) the institutionalized means for attaining them. The social structure, in Merton's formulation, distributes access to the legitimate means for attaining highly valued goals. Crime and deviance result, then, from the malintegration of elements within culture and from a similar lack of fit between culture and social structure.

In the first case, excessive cultural emphasis is placed on success goals, and correspondingly less emphasis is placed on the legitimate means for achieving the goals. In sociological terms, success goals are strongly *institutionalized.* They are widely and deeply internalized in the population and are accompanied by sharply etched images of successful persons or roles (for example, "the village elders" in some societies and "captains of industry" in others). Simply put, they are the goals that "everyone" knows about, that "everyone" thinks are important, and that "everyone" strives for. By contrast, the legitimate means to attain the goals are neither as well defined in society nor as salient to personal or collective action. Because they are not as strongly institutionalized, they lack the overwhelmingly and universally obligatory character of success goals. Considerable discretion is allowed in one's orientation to means, which implies greater tolerance for deviance from means than from goals. The greater the emphasis on goals relative to means, then, the stronger the pressure on persons to deviate from established modes of behavior, including legal standards, in the pursuit of culturally defined success.

The second way in which social organization produces crime, according to Merton, is by unequally distributing opportunities to achieve success goals in the population. Because of their privileged position in the social structure, by which Merton means primarily the class system, some persons or groups have advantages over others in the pursuit of success. Yet all are striving for the same goals. Social structure in this sense contradicts culture. Culture promises what social structure cannot deliver—success, for all. People faced with this contradiction between cultural mandate and structural impediment are subject to pressures or "strain" to abandon legal but ineffective means of goal attainment in favor of illegal, effective ones. These pressures are particularly acute, Merton argues, for members of the lower class, who lack access to the legitimate means of attaining the goals shared by members of all classes.

Both dimensions of social organization are thus fully implicated in Merton's explanation of crime. Unlike control theory, anomie theory emphasizes the importance of culture in the generation of crime and deviance. Unlike cultural learning theory, however, anomie theory does not assume that deviance is simply a matter of cultural definition or differential socialization. Anomie theory does not require the existence of deviant culture to explain deviant behavior. On the contrary, Merton proposes that criminal behavior results, in part, from conformity to conventional standards of success—but only in part. The great analytical advantage of anomie theory over alternative perspectives on crime is that it always calls attention back to the cultural and structural contexts of conformity to or deviation from conventional goals and means. Crime results when conformity to conventional success goals occurs in the context of a cultural overemphasis on ends relative to means and in the context of structural inequality of access to the approved means. Neither cultural conformity nor structural deprivation is, by itself, a sufficient cause of crime in Merton's formulation.

In light of common misinterpretations and misapplications of Merton's argument, it is important to underscore the point, as Merton does himself, that anomie theory is not a simple economic deprivation perspective on crime. Structural deprivation or inequality produces pressures to deviate under very specific cultural circumstances. Merton maintains that the relationship between deprivation and crime is high where there is great "cultural emphasis on monetary accumulation as a symbol of success," such as in the United States, and low where there is not.[38] In short, for Merton, culture conditions the impact of social structure on crime.[39] Less well developed in Merton's theory, yet equally important for explaining macrolevel variations in crime rates, is how social structure conditions or mediates the effect of culture on crime. We develop the latter point in detail in our discussion of the cultural and social sources of crime in the next chapter. However, before presenting our argument, which draws heavily on the anomie perspective, it is necessary to address some of the more important criticisms of anomie theory in general and of Merton's explanation of crime in the United States in particular.

Criticisms of Anomie Theory

Merton's formulation of the anomie perspective and his application of the perspective to the American crime problem have been heavily criticized. Some of the criticisms are, to be sure, friendly in nature and have served to expand and ultimately strengthen the theory by incorporating ideas from other perspectives. The most important of these are the contributions of Albert Cohen and Richard Cloward and Lloyd Ohlin.[40] Both contributions emphasize the importance of *subcultural adaptations* by lower- and working-class youth to the problem of limited access to legitimate opportunities for success. Neither fundamentally challenges the premises of cultural universalism and structural inequality that underlie the anomie perspective. The criminologist Francis Cullen has suggested that Cohen's and Cloward and Ohlin's works (the latter, in particular) represent a significant break with "stress" theories of deviant or criminal motivations, such as Merton's, in their emphasis on explaining the alternative forms deviant adaptations may assume under varying structural and cultural conditions.[41] However, as we pointed out earlier, the general idea that cultural adaptations arise under specific structural circumstances *and* that structural pressures are culturally mediated is consistent with Merton's view of the two components of social organization as variable and interactive—and is missing from cultural or control perspectives.

Many other criticisms of Merton's argument have been far less friendly. Four of these criticisms stand out as both important in their own right and highly relevant to the purposes of the present volume:[42]

1. Merton assumes that value consensus exists in society and that the goal of monetary success is supreme. In fact, other goals are equally important, if not more important, for many Americans, and no single value pattern dominates American culture.

2. Merton's formulation of the crime problem is class biased. His explanation cannot explain the crimes of the rich and powerful. Moreover, the high frequency of such crimes constitutes empirical disconfirmation of the theory.

3. Merton fails to draw out the radical policy implications of his argument; he erroneously implies that liberal social reform (that is, providing greater equality of opportunity) offers a realistic solution to the crime problem in the United States.

4. Finally, Merton does not provide a precise definition of anomie. Alternatively, the conception of anomie that is discernible in his theory differs significantly from, and is inferior to, Durkheim's original formulation.

The first of these criticisms is based, in our view, on a caricature of Merton's position. Merton does not assume complete value consensus, nor does he assert that monetary success is the only meaningful goal in American culture. To the contrary, he explicitly disavows such a simple-minded position, stating that it would be "fanciful to assert that accumulated wealth stands alone as a symbol of success."[43] Rather, his point is that monetary success enjoys a position of special prominence in the hierarchy of goals in the United States and serves as a common benchmark for determining achievement. This assumption strikes us as a very reasonable one, and ample evidence backs it up. Research on the social meanings of success reveals that material well-being is indeed the principal standard used in popular judgments of social standing in America.[44]

The criticism that anomie theory is class biased also reflects a somewhat oversimplified reading of Merton's arguments. It is true that Merton concentrates on the criminal behavior of the lower classes in explicating the implications of his theory for the social distribution of crime in American society. However, his basic argument can be extended to explain criminal behavior among those at the upper levels of the social hierarchy as well. A good illustration of this type of extension is provided in the recent work of Nikos Passas. Passas describes the strain toward anomie experienced by corporate executives, individuals who are under severe pressures to maximize profits under conditions of structural constraints. Such a situation, Passas suggests, is conducive to "organizational innovation"—high levels of corporate deviance and white-collar crime. Passas thus explains how both upper- and lower-class crimes can be accounted for by reference to the very same mechanisms, mechanisms that are described in the general anomie perspective.[45]

More important for present purposes, Merton's theory should not be reduced to his explanation of the social distribution of crime. Merton actually advances two related but distinct explanations of crime. One concerns the social distribution of crime within a society, but the other pertains to variation in levels of crime across societies. Although the former has received far greater attention than the latter from researchers and other theorists—and is the primary basis for the conversion of anomie theory into strain theory—the two explanations are in fact separable. This means that conceptual and empirical challenges to one are not necessarily damaging to the other. We draw most directly on those aspects of Merton's arguments that deal with variation in crime rates across rather than within societies, and hence the class-bias criticism is largely irrelevant to our analysis.[46]

In contrast, we find merit in the third criticism of Merton's thesis, that he and his followers fail to recognize fully the radical policy implications of the anomie perspective on crime. Merton often is faulted for being politically naive when considering the prospects for implementing greater equality of opportunity in American society. As Vold and Bernard remind us, "patterns of self-interest always develop around existing social structural arrangements," and those who benefit from the status quo are likely to resist efforts at social change and to have the political resources to do so effectively.[47]

In our view, however, a more fundamental criticism can be leveled at the liberal policy implications typically associated with Merton's theory: They do not really follow from the theory itself. If the American Dream places a heavy cultural emphasis on monetary success at any cost for everyone in society, then those who are unsuccessful in the pursuit of material well-being will be pressured to use illegitimate means regardless of the "openness" of the opportunity structure. The realization of a perfect meritocracy with full equality of opportunity would not eliminate the cultural pressures for crime. It would mainly redistribute the pressures to different individuals, those who lack the skills and talents that are rewarded in the marketplace.[48] Hence, expanding opportunities to disadvantaged segments of the population, however desirable in its own right, is not a crime reduction strategy that necessarily follows from Merton's theory.

The fourth criticism often leveled at Merton, that his use of the concept of anomie is not always clear, also has considerable merit. Anomie appears to have two distinct meanings in Merton's formulation. One is the rather standard reference to the weakening of the regulatory force of social norms, in other words, "normlessness." In this sense, anomie might be viewed as indicating the absence of culture. An alternative view, which has been formulated very effectively by Marco Orru, is that anomie is an important *product* of culture.[49] Specifically, anomie may be seen as a "value" to be inculcated along with others by the culture of modern capitalism—one that prescribes a high level of normative flexibility in the pursuit of dominant cultural goals. Both of these meanings of anomie are hinted at by Merton, and they are both also contained in Durkheim's earlier discussion of the anomic consequences of modernization.

The modern capitalist economy, Durkheim observed, is in a chronic state of deregulation. Industrialization removed traditional social controls on aspirations; the limitless and inherently frustrating pursuit of material and social rewards is now defined as morally obligatory. In his classic study *Suicide,* Durkheim writes:

> It is everlastingly repeated that it is man's nature to be eternally dissatisfied, constantly to advance, without relief or rest, toward an indefinite goal. The longing for infinity is daily represented as a mark of moral distinction.[50]

Anomie refers to the social conditions that characterize this "longing for infinity." They include not only the breakdown of traditional social controls, or the failure to replace them with new ones, but also new standards and symbols of personal achievement. For Durkheim, anomie is both the weakening of traditional moral regulation and a new kind of morality. It is the morality of modern capitalism—an open and peculiarly permissive morality, without doubt, but one that nevertheless functions to motivate conduct. Limitless achievement is not simply what is exposed by the removal of traditional social constraints; it is itself an "ethic" that must be culturally motivated and socially sustained. In sum, for both Merton and Durkheim the deregulation of behavior results not only from the passing of traditional society; it is part of the cultural context of capitalist society.

The fundamental question for Durkheim was whether modern societies could develop new forms of control to limit the very "appetites" that they helped to stimulate. He suggested specific institutional changes, such as the formation of occupational communities and the enhancement of the moral force of the state, to bring the new controls into being. This is where Merton makes his decisive break with Durkheim. Merton fails to extend his conception of social structure beyond the class system. The function of social structure, for Merton, is to distribute opportunities to achieve cultural goals. However, as Durkheim recognized, there is more to social structure than this. Social structure also functions to place limits on certain cultural imperatives so that they do not dominate and ultimately destroy others. This is the specific role of social institutions. However, Merton devotes little attention to institutions in his discussion of social structure and anomie.

The basic shortcoming remaining in Merton's explanation of crime, and in the anomie tradition more generally, is the absence of a comprehensive theory of institutional structure and functioning. The major purpose of the next chapter is to begin to fill this gap in the anomie tradition and, in so doing, to realize more fully the promise of the sociological paradigm.

NOTES

1. Short (1985, p. 51).

2. See Bailey (1987, pp. 24–26) for a discussion of the role of paradigms in social science.

3. See Short (1985) and Cohen (1985).

4. See Turk (1969) for an analysis of the general process of criminalization. See Gove, Hughes, and Geerken (1985) and O'Brien (1985) for general discussions of issues in the measurement of crime.

5. Durkheim defines "social facts" in *The Rules of Sociological Method* ([1895] 1964b). He applies the idea of social facts to what is commonly viewed as a quintessential individual act—the taking of one's own life—in his classic work *Suicide* ([1897] 1966).

6. The relationship between individual educational attainment and unemployment has been calculated by the authors using General Social Survey data from the Microcase analysis program. The data are for persons between the ages of eighteen and sixty-four. The data for aggregate educational characteristics refer to those who have completed four years or more of college (U.S. Bureau of the Census, 1994, p. 157, Table 232). The unemployment time series displayed in Figure 3–1 refers to the percentage of the civilian labor force unemployed in selected years between 1960 and 1993 (U.S. Bureau of

the Census, 1994, p. 396, Table 616). For a discussion of macrolevel unemployment trends, see Samuelson and Nordhaus (1989, Chapter 13).

7. Hodgins (1992, p. 482).

8. See Cohen (1985, pp. 230–231) for a general discussion of the interrelationships between individual- and macrolevel theorizing in criminology.

9. This conception of the seriousness of crimes is consistent with the approach taken by criminologists who have scaled different crime types according to their perceived seriousness based on ratings from general population surveys. See, for example, Rossi, Waite, Bose, and Berk (1974); Sellin and Wolfgang (1964); and Wolfgang, Figlio, Tracy, and Singer (1985).

10. Vold and Bernard (1986, p. 245). The classic statement of control theory is Travis Hirschi's *Causes of Delinquency* (1969). See also Kornhauser (1978).

11. See Burton and Cullen (1992, p. 8).

12. The influence of methodological choices and constraints on data acquisition and theory formulation in criminology, and on the development of the control perspective in particular, is revealed in an interview with Travis Hirschi: "Control theory as I stated it cannot really be understood unless one takes into account the fact that I was attached to a particular

method of research. When I was working on the theory, I knew that my data were going to be survey data; therefore I knew that I was going to have mainly the perceptions, attitudes, and values of individuals as reported by them....Had I data on other people, or on the structure of the community, I would have had to state the theory in a quite different way" (quoted in Lilly, Cullen, and Ball, 1989, p. 105). Stitt and Giacopassi (1992) speculate that the most likely reason for the dominance of social control theory in criminology is that "Hirschi's version was directly operationally defined in a survey format" (p. 4).

13. Rosenberg and Mercy (1986, p. 376). The discussion that follows draws from Rosenfeld and Decker (1993).

14. Centers for Disease Control (1991); Dobrin, Wiersema, Loftin, and McDowall (1996, p. 288, Table 4.37); Martinez-Schnell and Waxweiler (1989); U.S. Bureau of the Census (1994, p. 94, Table 126); U.S. Public Health Service (1990).

15. Gottfredson and Hirschi (1990).

16. Parsons (1951) characterizes culture as the "symbolic-meaningful" realm of social organization. The concept of a social institution is explained in Chapter 4.

17. See Bernard (1995), Cullen (1983), and Messner (1988).

18. In addition, we have excluded biophysiological perspectives from this discussion. See Fishbein (1990) and Wilson and Herrnstein (1985) for overviews of arguments and research on the relationship between biophysiological factors and criminality. Walters (1992) provides a systematic review of studies of the "gene-crime" relationship. Good discussions of the control, social learning, and strain perspectives can be found in Vold and Bernard (1986), Braithwaite (1989, pp. 16–43), and Lilly et al. (1989). Braithwaite (1989) includes labeling theory in his broad etiological framework for understanding crime and social control. Pfohl (1985) provides an excellent overview of labeling and conflict theories as well as etiological perspectives on crime and deviance.

19. Sutherland (1947, p. 7).

20. Sykes and Cullen (1992, p. 320n). In addition to Sutherland's theory of differential association, influential contributions to the cultural-social learning perspective include the reformulation of differential association theory in the terms of operant conditioning theory by Burgess and Akers (1966; see also Akers, Krohn, Lanza-Kaduce, and Radosevich 1979); Curtis's (1975) discussion of violent subcultures among urban blacks; the "Southern subculture of violence" hypothesis as developed by Gastil (1971) and Hackney (1969; see Hawley and Messner (1989) for a detailed overview of theory and research in this area); Miller's (1958) discussion of crime and lower-class culture; and Wolfgang and Ferracuti's (1967) classic statement of the "subculture of violence" thesis. Although not intended as an explanation of crime, but rather of the persistence of poverty, Oscar Lewis's (1966) idea of a "culture of poverty" figures importantly in criticisms of cultural deviance theory (see Kornhauser, 1978, pp. 10–12).

21. Kornhauser (1978, p. 196) has remarked, "In Sutherland's world rules are never willfully violated." Kornhauser's (1978) *Social Sources of Delinquency* and Hirschi's (1969) *Causes of Delinquency* remain the most important theoretical critiques of the cultural deviance perspective.

22. Kornhauser (1978, pp. 9–10).

23. van den Haag (1978, p. 210).

24. See Rosenfeld (1989, pp. 456–457).

25. See Hirschi (1969). This section draws heavily on Rosenfeld (1989, p. 457). The imagery of human nature underlying control theory—the "Hobbesian ontology"—is grounded in the classic contribution of Thomas Hobbes ([1651] 1958).

26. For a description of the Chicago School's analysis of urban social and ecological dynamics, see Park, Burgess, and McKenzie ([1925] 1967). See Shaw and McKay (1969) for a description of the sources and consequences of social disorganization in neighborhoods. Bursik and Grasmick refer to neighborhood criminology and neighborhood theories of crime in their study of community crime control (1993).

27. Good discussions of changes and continuities in disorganization theory include Bursik (1988), Bursik and Grasmick (1993),

Sampson and Groves (1989), and Stark (1987). One of the more important elaborations of the classical social disorganization perspective is "routine activities" theory. The central claim of this perspective is that opportunities for successful criminal victimization vary along with normal patterns of social interaction (for example, work and leisure). Crime occurs when motivated offenders come into contact with suitable targets (persons or property) in situations where "guardians" are unable to intervene to protect the targets of crime. See Cohen and Felson (1979).

28. See Mills (1943).

29. Kornhauser (1978, p. 13).

30. Kornhauser (1978, p. 13).

31. See Kroeber and Parsons (1958).

32. From the 1939 edition of Sutherland's textbook quoted in Vold and Bernard (1986, p. 212).

33. See Vold and Bernard (1986, pp. 212–213).

34. See Kornhauser (1978, pp. 62–82).

35. Three notable efforts to bring together different theories of crime within a single explanatory framework are the explanation of delinquency and drug use developed by Delbert Elliott and colleagues (Elliott, Huizinga, and Ageton, 1985); Hagan, Simpson, and Gillis's (1987) "power-control" explanation of gender and crime (see also Colvin and Pauly, 1983); and John Braithwaite's (1989) theory of crime and "reintegrative shaming." For a critique of attempts at theoretical synthesis or integration in criminology, see Hirschi (1979, 1989).

36. Kornhauser (1978, p. 69).

37. See Merton (1938; 1959; 1964; 1968, pp. 185–248).

38. Merton (1938, pp. 680–681).

39. See Messner (1988, pp. 47–49) for an elaboration of this point.

40. Cohen (1955) and Cloward and Ohlin (1960).

41. Cullen (1983, 1988).

42. Excellent discussions of these and related criticisms of Merton's theory may be found in Clinard (1964), Bernard (1984), Pfohl (1985, pp. 210–239), and Vold and Bernard (1986, pp. 185–204).

43. Merton (1968, p. 190).

44. See Rainwater (1974) and Coleman and Rainwater (1978).

45. Passas (1990). See also Cohen (1995) and Vaughn (1983).

46. See Messner (1988).

47. Vold and Bernard (1986, pp. 202–203).

48. See especially Vold and Bernard (1986, p. 203).

49. Orru (1987, pp. 142–143).

50. Durkheim ([1897] 1966, p. 257).

4

Culture, Institutional Structure, and Social Control: A Sociological Explanation of Crime

America has always been the most competitive of societies. It poises its citizens against one another, with the warning that they must make it on their own. Hence the stress on moving past others, driven by a fear of falling behind. No other nation so rates its residents as winners or losers.

ANDREW HACKER

TWO NATIONS: BLACK AND WHITE, SEPARATE, HOSTILE, UNEQUAL[1]

In August 1974, under threat of impeachment, Richard Nixon resigned from the office of president of the United States. Tom Wicker, in his book *One of Us: Richard Nixon and the American Dream*, speculates about the reasons for Nixon's continuing popularity, even after most Americans had been convinced of his crimes. Wicker suggests that Nixon may have represented a national self-assessment. Americans may have seen reflected in him

> their own melancholy knowledge, hard earned in a demanding world, that ideals had to yield to necessity, right to might, compassion to interest, principle to circumstance. They might even have understood that Nixon, or anyone, could believe himself forced on occasion to cheat a little, lie a little, find an edge, get out front of more favored competitors any way he could—as they themselves had done, or would do—in the unrelenting battles of life. . . . If, as president, he swore to uphold the Constitution but skirted it when he could, that was American still; which of us in the national rush to get ahead has never cut a corner or winked at the law?[2]

In Wicker's view, Nixon was not an American aberration but a reflection of fundamental features of American society.

Although his misdeeds were not motivated by economic concerns in the narrow sense, Nixon's actions and his character, Wicker suggests, are best understood in terms of the logic and language of the marketplace. In the "rush to get ahead," it is sometimes necessary to "find an edge," "cut a corner," bend "principle to circumstance," "cheat a little," "lie a little." These are actions and motivations that ordinary Americans can understand, if not condone, because they too inhabit the tough, competitive social terrain described by Tom Wicker and Andrew Hacker: a world of "unrelenting battles" in which the "fear of falling behind" drives combatants to adopt the survival ethic of "do unto others before they do unto you." Nixon's story, in short, is a paradigm of the social forces conducive to crime in the United States.

In this chapter, we explicate and illustrate these criminogenic forces, and in so doing we advance a sociological explanation for the high rates of crime in American society. Our basic thesis is that the American Dream itself exerts pressures toward crime by encouraging an anomic cultural environment, an environment in which people are encouraged to adopt an "anything goes" mentality in the pursuit of personal goals. Furthermore, we argue that the anomic pressures inherent in the American Dream are nourished and sustained by a distinctive *institutional balance of power* dominated by the economy. The interplay between the core cultural commitments of the American Dream and its companion institutional balance of power results in widespread anomie, weak social controls, and, ultimately, high levels of crime.

To develop these arguments, we begin this chapter with a detailed discussion of the value orientations underlying the American Dream and the ways in which this value complex is conducive to an anomic environment. We then discuss the nature of social institutions, the interdependencies among institutions, and the interrelationships between culture and institutional structure. Finally, we explore the consequences of the cultural and institutional organization of American society for levels and patterns of serious crime.

THE VALUE FOUNDATIONS OF THE AMERICAN DREAM

Robert Heilbroner has asked:

> Who has not reflected on the question of why the Japanese are so different from ourselves? Or the Swedes or the Italians, the French or the Germans? The answer that we give to this question is that their "cultures" are different, which indeed they are, but different in what ways?[3]

Robert Merton, in his essay "Social Structure and Anomie," provides a useful starting point for formulating an answer to Heilbroner's question about the distinctiveness of American culture. What sets the United States apart from other modern, industrial nations, according to Merton, is the cultural ethos of the American Dream. Merton himself does not provide a formal definition of the American Dream, but it is possible to formulate a reasonably concise characterization of this cultural orientation based on Merton's discussion of American culture in general, his scattered references to the American Dream, and the commentary of others on Merton's work.[4] Our definition, which we introduced in Chapter 1, is as follows: The American Dream refers to a commitment to the goal of material success, to be pursued by everyone in society, under conditions of open, individual competition.

The American Dream is a powerful force in our society because it embodies the basic value commitments of the culture: its achievement orientation, individualism, universalism, and peculiar form of materialism that has been described as the "fetishism of money."[5] Each of these value orientations contributes to the anomic character of the American Dream: its strong emphasis on the importance of realizing cultural goals in comparison with its relatively weak emphasis on the importance of using the legitimate means to do so.

Before examining the value complex underlying the American Dream, we caution against an overly simplistic interpretation of American culture. The United States is a complex and, in many respects, culturally pluralistic society. It neither contains a single, monolithic value system nor exhibits complete consensus surrounding specific value orientations. Historically, certain groups have been completely excluded from the American Dream. An obvious example is that of enslaved African Americans in the antebellum South. In addition, cultural prescriptions and mandates are filtered through prevailing gender roles. Indeed, we argue later in this chapter that the interpretation of the American Dream differs to some extent for men and women. We nevertheless concur with Jennifer Hochschild's claim that the American Dream has been, and continues to be, a "defining characteristic of American culture," a cultural ethos "against which all competitors must contend."[6] An adequate understanding of the crime problem in the United States, therefore, is impossible without reference to the cluster of values underlying the American Dream: achievement, individualism, universalism, and materialism.

Achievement

A defining feature of American culture is its strong achievement orientation. People are encouraged to make something of themselves, to set goals and to strive to reach them. To paraphrase the Army recruitment slogan, Americans are exhorted "to be all that they can be." At the same time, personal worth tends to be evaluated on the basis of the outcome of these efforts. Success, in other words, is to a large extent the ultimate measure of a person's value. As Marco Orru explains:

> The measure of individuals' social esteem is not provided by their position in the social system according to inherited status, to their location in social networks or to other ascribed traits; instead, one's own talents as measured

by individual achievement are the predominant (if not the only) standard of judgment.[7]

Given such a value orientation, the failure to achieve is readily equated with a failure to make any meaningful contribution to society at all. The cultural pressures to achieve at any cost are thus very intense. In this way, a strong achievement orientation, at the level of basic cultural values, is highly conducive to the mentality that "it's not how you play the game; it's whether you win or lose."[8]

Individualism

A second basic value orientation at the core of American culture is individualism. Americans are deeply committed to individual rights and individual autonomy. Bellah and his colleagues, in their book *Habits of the Heart*, describe the centrality of individualism to the American identity in these terms:

[Americans] believe in the dignity, indeed the sacredness, of the individual. Anything that would violate our right to think for ourselves, judge for ourselves, make our own decisions, live our lives as we see fit, is not only morally wrong, it is sacrilegious.[9]

This obsession with the individual, when combined with the strong achievement orientation in American culture, exacerbates the tendency toward anomie. In the pursuit of success, people are encouraged to "make it" on their own. Fellow members of society thus become competitors and rivals in the struggle to achieve social rewards and, ultimately, to validate personal worth. The intense individual competition to succeed pressures people to disregard normative restraints on behavior when these restraints threaten to interfere with the realization of personal goals.[10]

Universalism

A third basic value orientation in American culture is universalism. Socialization into the cultural goals of American society has a decidedly democratic quality. With few exceptions, everyone is encouraged to aspire to social ascent, and everyone is susceptible to evaluation on the basis of individual achievements. An important corollary of this universal entitlement to dream about success is that the hazards of failure are also universal. Because virtually no one is exempt from the cultural mandate for individual achievement, the anomic pressures associated with an individualistic achievement orientation permeate, albeit with varying degrees of intensity, the entire social structure.

The "Fetishism" of Money

Finally, in American culture success is signified in a distinctive way: by the accumulation of monetary rewards. Money is awarded special priority in American culture. As Merton observes, "In some large measure, money has been consecrated as a value in itself, over and above its expenditure for articles of consumption or its use for the enhancement of power." The point to empha-size here is not that Americans are uniquely materialistic, for a strong interest in material well-being can be found in most societies. Rather, the distinctive feature of American culture is the preeminent role of money as the "metric" of success. Orru succinctly expresses the idea in the following terms: "Money is literally, in this context, a *currency* for measuring achievement."[11]

There is an important implication of the signification of achievement with reference to monetary rewards. Monetary success is inherently open-ended. It is always possible in principle to have more money. Hence, the American Dream offers "no final stopping point." It requires "never-ending achieve-ment."[12] The pressure to accumulate money is therefore relentless, which en-tices people to pursue their monetary goals by any means necessary. A seventeen-year-old African American interprets Malcolm X's use of the ex-pression "by any means necessary" in just these materialistic terms:

> Malcolm is saying that it's about power. We can go to school and study and try to get power. Or we can take it and get violent if you push us to the edge. If we get jobs and money, we'll march your march and talk your talk. It's not a black-white thing, it's a green thing.

The media play a pivotal role in cultivating these anomic pressures associ-ated with a consumerist culture. As one social critic observes:

> Perhaps television's influence stems not from specific programming con-tent, but from its being a major component in the American, and indeed now the international, way of life. The commercial medium is designed to sell, everything from the audiences sought by advertisers to the expensive sneakers sought by youngsters, many of whom will do whatever is neces-sary to get them. They have been insistently persuaded that their lives are nothing without these athlete-sponsored products.[13]

In sum, the dominant value patterns of American culture—specifically, its achievement orientation, its competitive individualism, its universalism in goal orientations and evaluative standards, when harnessed to the preeminent goal of monetary success—crystallize into the distinctive cultural ethos of the American Dream. The American Dream, in turn, encourages members of so-ciety to pursue ends, in Merton's words, "limited only by considerations of technical expediency."[14] This open, widespread, competitive, and anomic quest for success provides a cultural environment highly conducive to criminal behavior.

Cultural forces thus play a prominent role in our explanation of the high levels of crime in American society. However, a complete sociological expla-nation of crime must extend beyond features of culture and incorporate social structural factors as well. Culture does not exist in isolation from social struc-ture but rather is expressed in, reproduced by, and occasionally impeded by, so-cial structure. Any comprehensive explanation that emphasizes "culture" as a cause of crime must therefore also consider the relevant range of structural conditions through which the cultural sources of crime are enacted. In our view, the most important of these structural conditions are the institutional arrangements of society.

THE INSTITUTIONAL STRUCTURE OF AMERICAN SOCIETY

In Chapter 2, we discussed the relationship between crime and what we referred to as "local institutions" without offering a formal definition of social institutions or a description of their functions at the level of entire social systems. Although this informal usage was appropriate for our descriptive purposes in that discussion, it is now necessary to define social institutions in a more rigorous way and to specify systematically the impact on crime of the institutional structure of society.

The Nature and Functioning of Social Institutions

Social institutions are the building blocks of whole societies. As such, they constitute the basic subject matter of macrolevel analysis. Institutions can be defined as "relatively stable sets of norms and values, statuses and roles, and groups and organizations" that regulate human conduct to meet the basic needs of a society.[15] Institutions are "accretive" social formations; they tend to develop slowly and continuously, seemingly without conscious purpose or design. They allow a society to endure over time despite the constant coming and going of individual members. In the words of the influential sociological theorist Talcott Parsons: "Institutional patterns are the 'backbone' of the social system."[16]

The functions of institutions in social systems have been compared with the functions of *instincts* in biological organisms: both channel behavior to meet basic system needs. However, as the sociologist Peter Berger has pointed out, this comparison reveals not only the functional equivalence but a basic structural difference between institutions and instincts. Human beings need institutions precisely because we cannot rely on "instinct" for complex social behavior. Compared to other species, humans are instinctually underdeveloped. Therefore, we must depend on institutions for our individual and collective survival. This institutional dependence has profound implications for the motivation and control of human social behavior, including criminal behavior.[17]

The basic social needs around which institutions develop include the need to (1) adapt to the environment, (2) mobilize and deploy resources for the achievement of collective goals, and (3) socialize members to accept the society's fundamental normative patterns.[18]

Adaptation to the environment is the primary responsibility of economic institutions. The *economy* consists of activities organized around the production and distribution of goods and services. It functions to satisfy the basic material requirements for human existence, such as the need for food, clothing, and shelter.

The political system, or *polity*, mobilizes and distributes power to attain collective goals. One collective purpose of special importance is the maintenance of public safety. Political institutions are responsible for "protecting members of society from invasions from without, controlling crime and disorder within, and providing channels for resolving conflicts of interest."[19] As part of the polity, agencies of the civil and criminal justice systems have major responsibility for crime control and the lawful resolution of conflicts.

The institution of the *family* has primary responsibility for the regulation of sexual activity and for the replacement of members of society. These tasks involve establishing and enforcing the limits of legitimate sexual relations among adults, the physical care and nurturing of children, and the socialization of children into the values, goals, and beliefs of the dominant culture. Families also bear much of the responsibility for the care of dependent persons in society more generally (for example, caring for the infirm and the elderly). In addition, a particularly important function of the family in modern societies is to provide emotional support for its members. To a significant degree, the family serves as a refuge from the tensions and stresses generated in other institutional domains. In this idea of the family as a "haven" from the rigors of the public world lies the implicit recognition of the need to counterbalance and temper the harsh, competitive conditions of public life.[20] These protective functions of the family traditionally have had greater salience for men. In addition, the family generates its own pressures and conflicts, and these have a special impact on women, the traditional caretakers of domestic life.

The institution of *education* shares many of the socialization functions of the family. Like the family, schools are given responsibility for transmitting basic cultural standards to new generations. In modern industrial societies, schools are also oriented toward the specific task of preparing youth for the demands of adult roles and, in particular, occupational roles. In addition, education is intended to enhance personal adjustment, facilitate the development of individual human potential, and advance the general knowledge base of the culture.

These four social institutions—the economy, the polity, the family, and education—are the central focus of our analysis of crime. They do not, of course, exhaust the institutional structure of modern societies, nor are they the only institutions with relevance to crime. Religion and mass communications, for example, have been the subject of important criminological research.[21] However, the economy, the polity, the family, and education are, in our view, central to what may be called an "institutional understanding" of crime.

Social institutions are to some extent distinct with respect to the primary activities around which they are organized. At the same time, however, the functions of institutions are overlapping and interdependent. The functioning of each institution has consequences for the functioning of the others. For example, the performance of the economy is dependent on the quality of the "human capital" cultivated in the schools. The capacity of the schools to develop human capital is circumscribed by the individual backgrounds that students bring with them from their families, what Pierre Bourdieu refers to as "cultural capital."[22] The effective functioning of all three of these institutions—the economy, education, and the family—presupposes an environment with at least a modicum of social order, for which the polity has formal responsibility. Finally, the effectiveness of the polity in promoting the collective good depends on the nature and quality of economic resources and human capabilities supplied by the other institutions.

The interdependence of major social institutions implies that, for the society to "work" at all, some coordination and cooperation must exist among institutions. The requirements for the effective functioning of any given institution, however, may conflict with the requirements of another. This potential for conflict is illustrated by the particularly stark contrast between the dominant values embodied in the institutions of the economy and the family. Family relationships are expected to be regulated by the norm of *particularism*, whereas transactions in the marketplace are supposed to be governed by *universalism*. Earl Babbie provides an amusing illustration of the distinction between these two value orientations:

> If you go into a supermarket to buy a loaf of bread, the various checkers are fundamentally interchangeable. You can purchase the bread equally well from any of the checkers, so you choose the check-out line that is the most convenient for you (for example, nearest, shortest).
>
> By contrast, suppose you are a parent with a young child in preschool. When you arrive at the classroom after the end of the school day, it would not be considered appropriate for you to simply pick up the most convenient child. Instead, you are expected to take a *particular* child home: *your own*.[23]

As this example suggests, economic life and family life are supposed to be governed by fundamentally different standards in modern industrial societies. Positions and roles in the family are allocated, in large measure, on the basis of ascribed characteristics. Each member is entitled to special considerations by virtue of his or her unique identity and place in the family unit. In contrast, economic relationships, such as transactions in the marketplace, are supposed to entail universalistic orientations, and economic positions are supposed to be filled according to achievement criteria. Persons who occupy the same or functionally equivalent statuses are to be treated similarly, and access to these statuses is supposed to be gained by demonstrating the capacity to perform successfully the associated duties and responsibilities. Thus, an inevitable tension arises between the kinds of value orientations required for the effective functioning of the family and those required for the efficient functioning of a market economy.[24]

Any given society therefore will be characterized by a distinctive arrangement of social institutions that reflects a balancing of the sometimes competing claims and requisites of the different institutions, yielding a distinctive institutional balance of power. Further, the nature of the resulting configuration of institutions is itself intimately related to the larger culture. Indeed, our basic premise about social organization is that culture and the institutional balance of power are mutually reinforcing. On the one hand, culture influences the character of institutions and their positions relative to one another. Culture is, in a sense, "given life" in the institutional structure of society. On the other hand, the patterns of social relationships constituting institutions reproduce and sustain cultural commitments. This is, ultimately, where culture "comes from."

We are well aware of the ideal typical nature of this description of institutional functioning. For example, occupational roles are often filled on the basis of functionally irrelevant criteria (such as race and gender), even in societies that proclaim open competition and equal opportunity for all members. Moreover, the persistence of ascriptive inequalities in societies formally committed to the norm of equal opportunity may give rise to feelings of injustice and dissatisfaction that promote criminal behavior. Our present concern, however, is not with how *departures* from cultural ideals influence crime rates but with how crime is produced when societies work pretty much the way they are supposed to.[25] In the section that follows, we discuss the type of institutional structure that is supportive of and compatible with the distinctive elements of American culture, an institutional structure characterized by the dominance of the economy.

The American Dream and the Institutional Balance of Power

The core elements of the American Dream—a strong achievement orientation, a commitment to competitive individualism, universalism, and, most important, the glorification of material success—have their institutional underpinnings in the economy. The most important feature of the economy of the United States is its capitalist nature. The defining characteristics of any capitalist economy are private ownership and control of property, and free-market mechanisms for the production and distribution of goods and services.

These structural arrangements are conducive to and presuppose certain cultural orientations. For the economy to operate efficiently, the private owners of property must be profit oriented and eager to invest, and workers must be willing to exchange their labor for wages. The motivational mechanism underlying these conditions is the promise of financial returns. The internal logic of a capitalist economy thus presumes that an attraction to monetary rewards as a result of achievement in the marketplace is widely diffused throughout the population.[26]

A capitalist economy is also highly competitive for all those involved, property owners and workers alike. Firms that are unable to adapt to shifting consumer demands or to fluctuations in the business cycle are likely to fail. Workers who cannot keep up with changing skill requirements or who are unproductive in comparison with others are likely to be fired. This intense competition discourages economic actors from becoming wedded to conventional ways of doing things and instead encourages them to substitute new techniques for traditional ones if they offer advantages in meeting economic goals. Therefore, a capitalist economy naturally cultivates a competitive, innovative spirit.

What is distinctive about the United States, however, is the *exaggerated* emphasis on monetary success and the *unrestrained* receptivity to innovation. The goal of monetary success overwhelms other goals and becomes the principal measuring rod for achievements. The resulting proclivity and pressures to innovate resist any regulation that is not justified by purely technical considerations. The obvious question that arises is: Why have cultural orientations that express the inherent logic of capitalism evolved to a particularly extreme degree in American society? The answer, we submit, lies in the inability of other social institutions to tame economic imperatives. In short, the institutional balance of power is tilted toward the economy.

The historical evidence suggests that this distinctive institutional structure has always existed in the United States. In his analysis of American slavery, the historian Stanley Elkins observes that capitalism emerged "as the principal dynamic force in American society," free to develop according to its own institutional logic without interference from "prior traditional institutions, with competing claims of their own." Whereas capitalism developed in European societies (and later in Japan) within powerful preexisting institutional frameworks, the institutional structure of American society emerged simultaneously with, and was profoundly shaped by, the requirements of capitalist economic development. American capitalism thus took on a "purity of form" unknown in other capitalist societies.[27] Moreover, other institutions were cast in distinctly subsidiary positions in relation to the economy.

In Elkins's view, by the 1830s many Americans could imagine that they had no need for "institutions" as such, which were regarded with suspicion as vestiges of an older, oppressive social order. Capitalism represented not a new type of social organization, in this view, but a liberation of the individual from social organization itself. The sources of social stability were to be found not in society but in human nature. The early American could believe that he did not

> draw from society his traditions, his culture, and all his aspirations; indeed he, the transcendent individual—the new symbol of virtue—now "confronted" society; he challenged it as something of a conspiracy to rob him of his birthright. Miraculously, all society then sprang to his aid in the celebration of that conceit.[28]

It is important to point out that Elkins's thesis does not support the simplistic assertion that "capitalism causes crime." Elkins himself calls attention to the fallacy in attributing the cultural and social characteristics of capitalist societies simply to the nature of capitalism:

> This idea cannot tell us much about the differences between two societies, both capitalist, but in one of which the "means of production" have changed into capitalistic ones and in the other of which the means of

production were never anything but capitalistic and in which no other forces were present to resist their development.[29]

Similarly, Robert Heilbroner writes that "*American* capitalism, not American *capitalism*" is responsible for the features of our society that distinguish it, for better or worse, from other capitalist societies.[30] As we documented in Chapter 2, serious crime rates in the United States are unusually high when compared with those in other modern capitalist societies. These differences, therefore, cannot be accounted for by capitalism alone. Variation in levels of crime and other aspects of these nations is rooted, following Elkins, in their contrasting institutional settings.

Elkins's portrait of the barren institutional landscape of early American society may be somewhat overdrawn, and aspects of his analysis of the North American slave system are controversial.[31] In addition, his account of the early American and "his" traditions, "his" culture, and "his" liberation from social organization refers quite literally to the free, white, male population of the United States at the time. Nonetheless, we accept the basic argument that capitalism developed in the United States without the institutional restraints found in other societies. As a consequence, the economy assumed an unusual dominance in the institutional structure of society from the very beginning of the nation's history, and this distinctive institutional arrangement has continued to the present.

Our notion of economic dominance in the institutional balance of power is similar to Elliot Currie's concept of a "market society" as distinct from a "market economy." According to Currie, in a market society "the pursuit of private gain becomes the organizing principle of all areas of social life—not simply a mechanism that we may use to accomplish certain circumscribed ends."[32] Economic dominance characteristic of the American market society is manifested, we argue, in three interrelated ways:

- devaluation of noneconomic institutional functions and roles,
- accommodation to economic requirements by other institutions, and
- penetration of economic norms into other institutional domains.

Devaluation   Noneconomic goals, positions, and roles are devalued in American society relative to the ends and means of economic activity. An example is the relative devaluation of the distinctive functions of education and of the social roles that fulfill these functions. Education is regarded largely as a means to occupational attainment, which in turn is valued primarily insofar as it promises economic rewards. Neither the acquisition of knowledge nor learning for its own sake is highly valued. A revealing illustration of the devaluation of education relative to purely monetary concerns is provided by an interview with a high school student whose grades dropped when she increased her schedule at her two after-school jobs to thirty hours a week. She described her feelings about the intrinsic rewards of education this way: "School's important but so's money. Homework doesn't pay. Teachers say education is your payment, and that just makes me want to puke."[33]

Given the relative devaluation of education, it is not surprising that effective performance of the roles involved with this activity does not confer particularly high status. The "good student" is not looked up to by his or her peers; the "master teacher" receives meager financial rewards and minimal public acclaim in comparison with those to be gained by success in business.

Similar processes are observed in the context of the family, although the tendency toward devaluation is perhaps not as pronounced as in other institutional arenas. There is a paradox here, because "family values" are typically extolled in public rhetoric. Nevertheless, family life has a tenuous position in American culture. It is the home *owner* rather than the home*maker* who is widely admired and envied—and whose image is reflected in the American Dream.

The lack of appreciation for the principal tasks of families—such as parenting, nurturing, and providing emotional support to others—is manifested in part in the low levels of compensation received by those who perform these tasks in the labor market. Consider the salaries for child-care providers. In 1992, the average weekly wages for full-time, in-home child-care workers was $154. This figure was about two-thirds that earned by bartenders—$251. Those working within the child-care field have expressed considerable frustration over their unsuccessful efforts to secure higher wages. In the words of one nanny interviewed by *Newsweek*, "People don't want to pay what it takes to hire someone qualified." Kelly Campbell, president of the International Nanny Association, is even more blunt in her criticism of the unwillingness of most Americans to provide child-care workers with decent wages. Campbell warns that "until we get to the point where we value our children as much as our material possessions, we're going to have problems with child care."[34]

The relative devaluation of the family in comparison with the economy is not an inevitable consequence of the emergence of a modern industrial society, whether capitalist or socialist. The comparative criminologist Freda Adler points to nations such as Bulgaria, the (then) German Democratic Republic, Japan, Saudi Arabia, and Switzerland to illustrate the possibilities for maintaining a strong commitment to the family despite the profound social changes that accompany the transformation from agriculturally based economies to industrial economies. Each of these countries has made extensive and sometimes costly efforts to preserve the vitality of the family. Furthermore, these are precisely the kinds of societies that exhibit low crime rates and are not, in Adler's words, "obsessed with crime."[35]

The distinctive function of the polity, providing for the collective good, also tends to be devalued in comparison with economic functions. The general public has little regard for politics as an intrinsically valuable activity and confers little social honor on the role of the politician. Indeed, the label "politician" is commonly used in a disparaging way. Perhaps as a result, average citizens are not expected to be actively engaged in public service, which is left to those with a "career" in politics. The contrast with economic activity is illuminating. The citizen who refuses to vote may experience mild social disapproval; the able-bodied adult who refuses to work is socially degraded. Economic participation is obligatory for most adults. In contrast, even the minimal form of political participation entailed in voting (which has more in common with shopping than with work) is considered discretionary, and useful primarily to the extent that it leads to tangible economic rewards (for instance, lower taxes).

The very purpose of government tends to be conceptualized in terms of its capacity to facilitate the individual pursuit of economic prosperity. A good illustration is the advice given to the Democratic ticket in the 1992 presidential campaign by the conservative columnist George Will. Will chastised liberal Democrats for their alleged preoccupation with issues of rights based on ethnicity and sexuality and advised the Democratic candidates to remember the following point that two popular former presidents, Franklin Roosevelt and Ronald Reagan, understood very well: "Americans are happiest when pursuing happiness, happiness understood as material advancement, pursued with government's help but not as a government entitlement."[36]

Will's advice to liberal Democrats is revealing, not only of the core content of the American Dream and its effect on popular views of government but of a particular kind of collective "right" to which Americans are entitled: the right to consume.[37] Both of the major political parties celebrate the right to acquire material possessions; they differ mainly with respect to the proper degree of governmental involvement in expanding access to the means of consumption. No matter which party is in power, the function of government, at least in the domestic sphere, remains subsidiary to individual economic considerations.

Interestingly, one distinctive function of the polity does not appear to be generally devalued, namely, crime control. There is widespread agreement among the American public that government should undertake vigorous efforts to deal with the crime problem. If anything, Americans want government to do more to control crime. Yet this apparent exception is compatible with the claim of economic dominance. Americans' obsession with crime is rooted in fears that crime threatens, according to political analyst Thomas Edsall, "their security, their values, their rights, and their livelihoods and the competitive prospects of their children." President Clinton used similar language when urging Congress to pass anticrime legislation in 1994. In his weekly radio address, Clinton warned that, unless the rise in crime is halted, "we can't exercise the opportunities that there are for us, and our children can't inherit the American dream."[38] In other words, because crime control bears directly on the pursuit of the American Dream, this particular function of the polity receives high priority.

Accommodation A second way in which the dominance of the economy is manifested is in the *accommodations* that emerge in those situations where institutional claims are in competition. Economic conditions and requirements typically exert a much stronger influence on the operation of other institutions than vice versa. For example, family routines are dominated by the schedules, rewards, and penalties of the labor market. Whereas parents worry about "finding time" for their families, few workers must "find time" for their

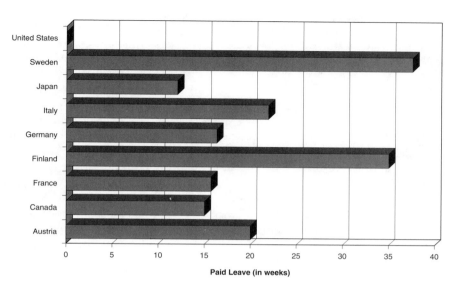

FIGURE 4–1 Family Leave in Nine Industrial Nations

jobs. On the contrary, many feel fortunate that the economy has found time for them.

Consider the resistance to parental leave in the United States. In a comprehensive review of the efforts of other nations to make child rearing compatible with the demands of the workplace, Vanderkolk and Young observe that "the U.S. trails significantly in the amount of help—or perhaps its value—granted to workers who are also new mothers." Only 5 percent of all employers offer paid parental leave in the United States. Most other industrialized nations, in contrast, mandate paid maternity or parental leave by law. Comparative data on minimum standards for paid parental or maternity leave are depicted in Figure 4–1, revealing the atypical status of the United States.[39] After a long political struggle, legislation on family and emergency leave was finally signed into law in the United States in 1993. Yet even this legislation only sets minimum standards for *unpaid*, but not paid, leave.

Most European nations implement additional policies that reflect a strong commitment to the institution of the family. These include direct cash allowances to families to cover some of the costs of child rearing, public child care for young children, and universal access to health care to deal with the special needs of the very young and the elderly. In Italy, such policies are considered part of a mother's "birthright."[40] The contrast between the United States and another capitalist society with very low crime rates, Japan, is particularly striking in this regard. In Japan, business enterprises are accommodated to the needs of the family, becoming in some respects "surrogate families," with services ranging from child rearing to burial.[41]

The most important way that family life is influenced by the economy, however, is through the necessity for paid employment to support a family.

Joblessness makes it difficult for families to remain intact or even to form in the first place. In the urban underclass, where rates of joblessness are chronically high, so too are rates of separation, divorce, single-parent households, and births to unmarried women.[42]

Educational institutions are also more likely to accommodate to the demands of the economy than is the economy to respond to the requirements of education. The timing of schooling reflects occupational demands rather than intrinsic features of the learning process or personal interest in the pursuit of knowledge. People go to school largely to prepare for "good" jobs. And once they are in the labor market, there is little opportunity to pursue further education for its own sake.

When workers do return to school, it is almost always to upgrade skills or credentials to keep pace with job demands, to seek higher-paying jobs, or to "retool" during spells of unemployment. A college admissions director observes that returning students are "hungry for practical education that they can take back to their workplace the next day." His university accommodates this demand by scheduling classes on Saturday, during the evening, and in shortened eight-week terms to ensure that education interferes as little as possible with students' work lives.[43]

At the organizational level, schools are dependent on the economy for financial resources. Private business is increasingly looked on as a savior of financially strapped public school systems.[44] To the extent that the viability of schools relies on the private sector, it is critical for school officials to convince business leaders that education is suitably responsive to business needs.

The polity likewise is dependent on the economy for financial support. Governments must accordingly take care to cultivate and maintain an environment hospitable to investment. If they do not, they run the risk of being literally "downgraded" by financial markets, as happened to Detroit in 1992 when Moody's Investors Service dropped the city's credit rating to noninvestment grade. Cities have little choice but to accommodate to market demands in such situations. In the words of a reporter for the *New York Times*: "A city proposes, Moody's disposes. There is no appeals court or court of last ratings resort."[45] The pursuit of the collective good is thus circumscribed by the imperatives of the private economy.

Penetration A final way in which the dominance of the economy in the institutional balance of power is manifested is in the *penetration* of economic norms into other institutional areas. Schools rely on grading as a system of extrinsic rewards, like wages, to ensure compliance with goals. In some schools, the connection between academic performance and earnings is literal: students are paid for completing assignments and for achieving high grades. For example, in the Learning by Earning program, children are paid $2 after reading a book and answering questions about it.[46] More generally, learning takes place within the context of individualized competition for external rewards, and teaching becomes oriented toward testing. Economic terminology also permeates the very language of education, as in the recent emphasis on "accountability" conceptualized in terms of the "value added" to students in the educational production process and the emphasis on students themselves as "products."[47]

Education itself is increasingly viewed as a commodity, no different from other consumer goods. A telling illustration of this trend is the recent innovation by some colleges of issuing warranties similar to a manufacturer's guarantee to accompany their diplomas. Neal Raisman, president of Rockland Community College, explains the rationale for this practice as follows: "We tell the public, 'Give us money, and we will guarantee you nothing.' I would never buy a toaster like that!"[48]

Within the polity, a "bottom-line" mentality develops. Effective politicians are those who deliver the goods. Moreover, the notion that the government would work better if it were run more like a business continues to be an article of faith among large segments of the American public. Many Americans in fact seem to prefer business leaders over public officials to perform key political functions. It is thus not surprising that successful businessman Peter Ueberroth was selected to head the "Rebuild L.A." task force established after the 1992 riot in south central Los Angeles, even though his prior business experience would seem to provide questionable preparation for the challenge of overcoming deep-seated social problems.

The most striking recent illustration of the mystique of the successful business leader as political savior is Ross Perot, who ran a remarkably successful presidential campaign in 1992 despite never having served in political office. Perot actually pointed to his lack of political experience with pride, explaining in particular that he had no experience running up massive deficits. Perot's impressive support as a third party candidate suggests that his repeated promise to run government more like a business was enthusiastically received by a large segment of the American public.

The family has probably been most resistant to the intrusion of economic norms. Yet even here, pressures toward penetration are apparent. Contributions to family life tend to be measured against the all-important breadwinner role, which has been extended to include women who work in the paid labor force. No corresponding movement of men into the role of homemaker has occurred. Here again, shifts in popular terminology are also instructive. Husbands and wives are "partners" who "manage" the household "division of labor" in accordance with the "marriage contract." We are aware of few comparable shifts in kin-based terminology, or primary group norms, from the family to the workplace.[49]

In sum, the social organization of the United States is characterized by a striking dominance of the economy in the institutional balance of power. As a result of this economic dominance, the inherent tendencies of a capitalist economy to orient the members of society toward an unrestrained pursuit of economic achievements are developed to an extreme degree. These tendencies are expressed at the cultural level in the preeminence of the competitive, individualistic pursuit of monetary success as the overriding goal—the American Dream—and in the relative deemphasis placed on the importance of using normative means to reach this goal—anomie. The anomic nature of the American Dream and the institutional structure of American society are thus mutually supportive and reinforcing. In the next section, we turn to the implications of this type of social organization for crime.

SOCIAL ORGANIZATION AND CRIME

Anomie and the Weakening of Institutional Control

Both of the core features of the social organization of the United States—culture and institutional structure—are implicated in the genesis of high levels of crime. At the cultural level, the dominant ethos of the American Dream stimulates criminal motivations while at the same time promoting a weak normative environment (anomie). At the institutional level, the dominance of the economy in the institutional balance of power fosters weak social control. And, as just explained, both culture and institutional structure are themselves interdependent. These interconnections between culture, social structure, and crime are presented schematically in Figure 4–2.

The cultural stimulation of criminal motivations derives from the distinctive content of the American Dream. Given the strong, relentless pressure for everyone to succeed, understood in terms of an inherently elusive monetary goal, people formulate wants and desires that are difficult, if not impossible, to satisfy within the confines of legally permissible behavior. This feature of the American Dream helps explain criminal behavior with an instrumental character, behavior that offers monetary rewards. This type of behavior includes white-collar offenses, street crimes such as robbery and drug dealing, and other crimes that occur as a consequence of these activities.

At the same time, the American Dream does not contain within it strong injunctions against substituting more effective, illegitimate means for less effective, legitimate means in the pursuit of monetary success. To the contrary, the distinctive cultural message accompanying the monetary success goal in the American Dream is the devaluation of all but the most technically efficient means. This anomic orientation leads not simply to high levels of crime in general but to especially violent forms of economic crime, for which the United States is known throughout the industrial world, such as mugging, carjacking, and home invasion.

Of course, the American Dream does not completely subsume culture. Other elements of culture affirm the legitimacy of legal prohibitions and the desirability of lawful behavior. In principle, these other elements of culture could counterbalance the anomic pressures emanating from the American Dream. However, the very same institutional dynamics that contribute to the pressures to "innovate" in the pursuit of economic goals also make it less likely that the anomic pressures inherent in the American Dream will in fact be counterbalanced by other cultural forces.

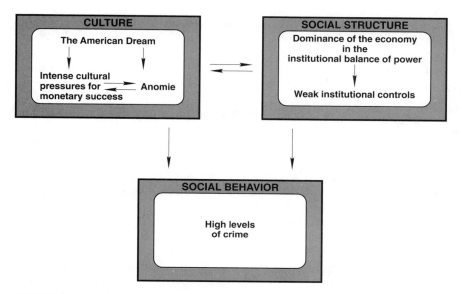

FIGURE 4–2 An Analytical Model of the Linkages Between Macrosocial Organization and Crime

Prosocial cultural messages tend to be overwhelmed by the anomic tendencies of the American Dream because of the dominance of the economy in the institutional balance of power. A primary task for noneconomic institutions such as the family and schools is to inculcate beliefs, values, and commitments other than those of the marketplace. But as these noneconomic institutions are relatively devalued and forced to accommodate to economic considerations, as they are penetrated by economic standards, they are less able to fulfill their distinctive socialization functions successfully. Sociologist Robert Bellah and his colleagues have made essentially the same point in their critique of the institutional structure of contemporary American society: "Economic institutions have invaded other institutions (politics, religion, family, etc.), making it harder for them to do what they were originally intended to do."[50]

Impotent families and schools are severely handicapped in their efforts to promote allegiance to social rules, including legal prohibitions. In the absence of strong socializing influences from these noneconomic institutions, the cultural message that comes through with greatest force is the one most compatible with the logic of the economy: the competitive, individualistic, and materialistic message of the American Dream. The anomie associated with this cultural ethos thus tends to neutralize and overpower normative restraints more generally, and the selection of the means for realizing *goals of any type*, not simply monetary goals, tends to be guided mainly by considerations of technical expediency.

This generalized anomie ultimately explains, in our view, the unusually high levels of gun-related violence in the United States. In the final analysis, guns are very effective tools for enforcing compliance. The American penchant for owning guns and using them reflects, in other words, a more general anomic cultural orientation, a willingness to pursue goals by any means necessary.

The basic social organization of the United States contributes to high levels of crime in another way. Institutions such as the family, schools, and the polity bear responsibility not only for socialization, and hence the normative control associated with culture, but also for the more external type of social control associated with social structure. External control is achieved through the active involvement of individuals in institutional roles and through the dispensation of rewards and punishments by institutions.

Social relationships within institutions are inevitably somewhat constraining for individuals. Indeed, the very concept of institutional "roles" implies restraint. Roles consist of behavioral expectations attached to social statuses, and thus the enactment of social roles implies that an individual's behavior is governed, at least to some extent, by constraints external to the individual. However, to the degree that noneconomic institutions are relatively devalued, the attractiveness of the roles that they offer for members of society is diminished. There is, accordingly, widespread detachment from these institutions and weak institutional control.

Economic roles, in contrast, are not culturally devalued but extolled. Yet the lack of restraint associated with detachment from noneconomic institutions is not effectively counterbalanced by economic controls. Institutions vary with respect to the extent to which they impose restraints on individuals, and the nature of this variation reflects the larger culture. In American society, the economy is an institution that by design is much less constraining than other institutions. It is a free-market economy, governed by the principle of laissez-faire. Ironically, then, Americans tend to be most strongly attached to the institution with the least restraining qualities—the economy. A lack of control at the level of institutional relationships thus parallels and complements the lack of control at the cultural level of social norms.

The relative impotence of noneconomic institutions also implies that they are limited in the incentives and penalties that they can offer for socially prescribed or proscribed behavior. For example, the government is constrained in its capacity to mobilize collective resources, including moral resources, to deter criminal choices. Single-parent families or those in which both parents have full-time jobs, all else equal, are less able to provide extensive supervision over children and to respond to behavior with consistent rewards and punishments.[51] All families must rely to some extent on other institutions, usually the schools, for assistance in social control. Yet poorly funded or crowded schools also find it difficult to exert effective supervision, especially when students see little or no connection between what is taught in the classroom and what is valued outside of it.

Finally, weak institutions invite challenge. Under conditions of extreme competitive individualism, people actively resist institutional control. Not only do they fall from the insecure grasp of powerless institutions, sometimes they deliberately, even proudly, push themselves away. The problem of *external* control by major social institutions, then, is inseparable from the problem of the *internal* regulatory force of social norms, or anomie. Anomic societies will inevitably find it difficult and costly to exert social control over the behavior of people who feel free to use whatever means prove most effective in reaching personal goals. Hence, the very sociocultural dynamics that make American institutions weak also enable and entitle Americans to defy institutional controls. If Americans are exceptionally resistant to social control—and therefore exceptionally vulnerable to criminal temptations—it is because they live in a society that enshrines the unfettered pursuit of individual material success above all other values. In the United States, anomie is considered a virtue.

The Social Distribution of Crime: Gender and Race

Thus far, we have described anomic pressures that derive from the basic social organization of American society. The intensity and pervasiveness of these pressures help explain the high crime rates in the United States in comparison with other advanced societies. It is also important, however, to ask whether the theoretical framework we have proposed for explaining the distinctive position of the United States when considered in international perspective can also account for the social distribution of crime within the nation. We believe that the logic of our argument is compatible with observed differences in crime rates across social categories in American society. Specifically, it helps account for two of the most striking observations about the social correlates of crime: the comparatively low rates of offending for females, and the comparatively high rates of offending for African Americans.

A wide range of evidence supports the claim that females are less involved in serious crime than are men. This pattern is reflected consistently in official arrest statistics, victimization surveys, and self-reports of criminal activity.[52] An important reason for this gender differential, we suggest, is that females are much more engaged than are males in a key social institution: the family.

Women usually perform the bulk of family tasks. They typically do more of the housework than men, spend more time on child care, and devote more time and effort to monitoring the well-being of marital relationships. Middle-aged daughters are also more likely than sons to provide services and support to aging parents. Even when women work in the paid labor force, they continue to bear primary responsibility for marriage, housework, parenthood, and kinship networks.[53]

This greater engagement in family life should lead to somewhat different cultural orientations for females in comparison with males, given the general logic of our argument about the interdependency between institutional roles and culture. Females should be less likely to exhibit unqualified support for the values associated with economic achievement and more likely to balance economic values with other values consistent with familial roles. In other words, men and women should interpret the American Dream somewhat differently. The commitment to materialism and individualistic competition—values associated with the market economy—should be weaker among females than among males. On the other hand, a value preference indicating a willingness to restrain self-interest out of concern for others, which is indispensable to the enactment of familial roles, should be stronger for females than for males.

Such gender differences in value orientations have in fact been documented in the literature. In a study of nationally representative samples of U.S. high school seniors spanning the period from the mid-1970s to the early 1990s, sociologists Ann Beutel and Margaret Mooney Marini report that male respondents are significantly more likely than female respondents to embrace the values of a market economy: "making profits, material acquisition, and competition." On the other hand, female students are more likely to express compassion and indicate a willingness to forego personal rewards to assist others who are in need. Similar gender differences have been observed for adult men and women in their orientations towards jobs. Women place a comparatively strong emphasis on the importance of being able to help others, and they are less likely to demonstrate a competitive orientation. In addition, females are significantly more likely than males to rate having children as an important personal goal.[54] Females, in other words, are more fully socialized into an institutional logic independent of that of the economy. As a result, we suggest that the anomic pressures of the American Dream are somewhat tempered for women, and their lesser involvement in crime is theoretically explainable.[55]

How long such institutional insulation from criminogenic pressures will last is an open question, especially given the increasing economic pressures that impinge on the family. There is no magical permanence in the tie between women and the family. Indeed, some anthropologists have claimed that the spell of the procreative and familial imperative has finally broken for large numbers of women as well as men. Managing a family and two full-time jobs imposes enormous strains on both women and men, but especially on women, and threatens the stability of marital and family bonds. Marriage and family are threatened even more by recent declines in manufacturing jobs, wages, and employment security. Middle- and working-class families bear the brunt of the former trend toward "the second shift"—a job both in the marketplace and at home.[56] The poor, particularly the urban underclass, have been hit hardest by increasing joblessness. Without greater insulation of the family itself from the pressures emanating from the economy, the inhibiting effects of extensive familial involvement on crime might very well diminish in the years ahead, and the crime rates of men and women could begin to converge.[57]

The institution of the family also figures importantly in the relationship between race and crime. As documented in Chapter 2, African Americans are disproportionately involved as victims and as offenders in conventional criminal activity. Although they do not fully account for the dominance of the

United States in international crime rankings, race differences in criminal offending within the nation are large and persistent. They are especially pronounced for violent crimes. Racial bias in the criminal justice system has not disappeared, but it does not explain the differential criminal involvement of African Americans.[58] That disproportionate involvement results, we suggest, from broader cultural and structural conditions.

The explanation we offer for the "overinvolvement" of African Americans in crime is essentially the mirror image of that we presented for the "underinvolvement" of women. We have argued that the lower level of crime among women is related to gender differences in noneconomic roles and responsibilities. Women's stronger connection with the family, in particular, insulates them to some degree from the full force of anomic cultural pressures. For a segment of the African American community, this pattern of cultural insulation and structural engagement is reversed: Family ties are tenuous for many young black men living in U.S. inner cities, leaving them fully exposed to the promise and pitfalls of the American Dream.

Any discussion of the role of the family in the African American community must acknowledge its durability and vitality in the face of persisting structural disadvantage. The black family survived the horrors of forced emigration to America, the brutalities of slavery, and the routine privations and frequent violence of Jim Crow segregation. Yet, what the slave system and its aftermath could not destroy is under siege by the "urban plantation" of the inner-city ghetto.[59] The family has not disappeared in inner-city communities, but the roles of men as husbands, fathers, and helpmates have been attenuated. The sources of change in the structure of the inner-city family are part of larger patterns of structural dislocation, including elevated levels of joblessness, highly concentrated poverty, and persistent racial segregation.[60] In other words, the tenuous connection between men and families in the inner city reflects an even broader institutional estrangement. Based on the logic of our explanation of crime, weakened institutional support and control are, in turn, associated with high levels of criminal involvement.

Crime in the inner city, however, is not simply a function of the alienation of young black men from the major institutions of the larger society. It is, just as important, a consequence of the assimilation of black Americans to mainstream cultural patterns, including the American Dream. Black and white Americans disagree on many things, but they are united in their commitment to the core tenets of the dominant success ideology. Large majorities of blacks and whites tell survey researchers that "the American Dream [is] alive today" and agree with the statement that it has "real meaning for you personally." Blacks are optimistic about their own and their children's mobility opportunities, and where the races do diverge somewhat in their views of success, "blacks are always the more confident." Moreover, depending on the particular survey or question, poor blacks are as likely or more likely than those in the middle class to endorse the American Dream as a highly desirable cultural prescription and as a realistic description of their personal experience.[61]

This strong affirmation of the American Dream by black Americans has had fateful consequences for the institutional life of black communities. On the one hand, without question the promise of economic opportunity and reward has provided generations of African Americans with the hope and determination necessary to endure oppressive and degrading social conditions. It is a wonder under the circumstances that so many have, in Hochschild's expression, remained "under the spell" of the American Dream for so long. On the other hand, African Americans have paid a high price for their commitment to the dominant success ideology. The anomic tendencies within the Dream—the emphasis on material success by any means necessary—have inflamed the consumption desires of inner-city children and adolescents, creating a "commodity worship" that even the strongest institutions would have difficulty keeping under control. At the same time, however, the anomic ethic threatens those institutions charged with taming the self-regarding behaviors stimulated by consumption. The toll on the inner-city family has been especially heavy. In a recent ethnographic study of a poor neighborhood in Philadelphia, Carl Husemoller Nightingale describes the reaction of inner-city boys to their parents' unsuccessful efforts to fulfill the boys' consumption cravings:

> Boys' desires to consume conspicuously and their judgments, based on mainstream standards, about their parents' abilities as providers led to doubts about the legitimacy of the parents' control. . . . For kids, the experience of living in a poor family amid a mass culture of abundance quickly sours their attitudes toward cooperation. . . . Parents' inability to provide the basic amenities of childhood 'as seen on tv,' their occasional wishful, desperate promises to the contrary, and their kids' memories of disappointment help forge a set of cynical assumptions about other people's motives in general, a first step toward the sense that one must manipulate and hustle in order to get what one desires.[62]

Although they are felt most acutely within the family, the anomic forces of the dominant culture have invaded other inner-city institutions as well. If left unchecked, they produce with disturbing frequency the scenes of institutional collapse and personal anguish depicted in Chapter 2. This prompts a final question for our analysis of crime in American society: What kinds of cultural and social changes are required to reduce the high levels of crime in American society? In the next chapter, we address the limitations of conventional crime control strategies and propose alternative directions for change that are consistent with our explanation of the anomic consequences of the American Dream.

NOTES

1. Hacker (1992, p. 29).

2. Wicker (1991, pp. 686–687).

3. Heilbroner (1991, pp. 538–539).

4. In our analysis of the value foundations of the American Dream, we rely heavily on Marco Orru's (1990) excellent exegesis of Merton's theory. Characterizations of this cultural ethos that are very similar to ours also can be found in studies of the "success theme" in American literature cited in Chapter 1. See Hearn (1977) and Long (1985).

5. The reference to the "fetishism of money" is from Taylor, Walton, and Young's (1973, p. 94) insightful discussion of Merton's theory of anomie.

6. Hochschild (1995, p. xi). Turner and Musick (1985) similarly emphasize the degree of consensus over "basic values" in contemporary American society. See Lemert (1964) for a critique of the view that modern societies exhibit value consensus.

7. Orru (1990, p. 234).

8. See in this regard Gouldner's (1970, p. 65) arguments concerning the tendency for "bourgeois utilitarian culture," of which American culture is a prime example, to place a "great stress upon winning or losing, upon success or failure as such."

9. Bellah, Madsen, Sullivan, Swidler, and Tipton (1985, p. 142).

10. Derber (1992, 1996) identifies an unrestrained and a degraded individualism as the primary cause of a "wilding epidemic" in America. He maintains that this epidemic is ultimately responsible for both criminal behavior and legal, egoistic behavior (for example, careerists who betray colleagues to advance their careers). Whereas Derber emphasizes the degeneration of the social order as the source of crime, which is reflected in his use of the metaphor of societal "illness," our perspective locates the causes of crime in the *normal* operations of the social system.

11. The first quotation is to Merton (1968, p. 190); the second is to Orru (1990, p. 235). See Schwartz (1994b, pp. 55–113)

for further discussion of the tendency for economic success to become "the measure of all things" in the professions, sports, and other areas of American life.

12. The references to "no final stopping point" and "never-ending achievement" are from Merton (1968, p. 190) and Passas (1990, p. 159), respectively.

13. The African American youth is quoted in Wilkerson (1992, p. B7). The quotation on the role of the media is from O'Connor (1993).

14. Merton (1968, p. 189).

15. Bassis, Gelles, and Levine (1991, p. 142). Our discussion of institutions draws heavily on this source. See also the incisive discussion of the normative significance of social institutions in Bellah et al. (1991, Chapter 1 and appendix).

16. Parsons (1964, p. 239).

17. See Berger (1963, pp. 87–91).

18. Our discussion of the needs fulfilled by institutions is based on Parsons's (1951) classic description of the functional requisites of social systems. Parsons identifies a fourth system need, the need to "integrate" the system around its core value orientations, and he locates the legal system within this functional realm. We follow the more common practice of treating the legal system, specifically criminal justice organizations and processes, as part of the political system. The "functionalism" associated with Parsons has been harshly criticized in the sociological literature in recent decades. A good review of the important controversies is provided by Downes and Rock (1982), who observe that critics of functionalism often attack absurdly "vulgarized" formulations of the perspective (p. 75). We concur with these authors' general conclusion that although functionalists may have "overplayed their hand, . . . at least they are playing the right sort of game" (p. 93).

19. Bassis et al. (1991, p. 142).

20. Lasch (1977).

21. See Stark, Kent, and Doyle (1982) on the relationship between religion and

delinquency. Surette (1992) provides a good overview of research on the mass media, crime, and justice.

22. Cited in MacLeod (1987, pp. 11–14).

23. Babbie (1992, p. 41).

24. The classic discussion of basic value patterns governing the orientation of actors in social situations is Parsons (1951).

25. See Blau and Blau (1982) and Messner and Golden (1992) for arguments about the relationship between ascriptive inequality and criminal violence. The premise that deviance can be understood with reference to the normal workings of societal institutions is characteristic of the general functionalist approach in sociology. See, in particular, Wright and Hilbert (1980).

26. Passas (1990, pp. 158–159). Polanyi ([1944] 1957) argues convincingly that this orientation of economic activity around the self-interested pursuit of profit and gain is not an inevitable, "natural" feature of the human species. Rather, it is unique to capitalist societies.

27. Elkins (1968, p. 43).

28. Elkins (1968, p. 33).

29. Elkins (1968, p. 43n).

30. Heilbroner (1991, pp. 539–540).

31. See Lane (1971).

32. Also consistent with our general argument, Currie observes that "the United States has long been the most market-dominated of Western industrial countries, the one with the least developed alternatives to the values and institutions of the market." Both quotations are from Currie (1991, p. 255). For a classic discussion of the tendency for markets to dominate other institutions in capitalist societies, and the dangers of this tendency, see Polanyi ([1944] 1957).

33. Waldman and Springen (1992, p. 81).

34. Beck (1993, p. 68).

35. Adler (1983, p. 131).

36. Will (1992).

37. See Edsall (1992, p. 10).

38. Edsall (1992, p. 9); New York Times (1994).

39. The quotation and the data on family leave are from Vanderkolk and Young (1991, pp. 160–161).

40. The reference to Italian mothers' "birthright" is from Bohlen (1996, p. 1), who also describes family leave and related support policies in other European nations. See also Vanderkolk and Young (1991, p. 13).

41. Adler (1983, p. 132). Japanese businesses also place a higher priority on providing jobs for their employees than on customer satisfaction and shareholder interests. As Friedman (1996, p. E15) explains, "The Japanese understand that a job gives dignity and stability to people's lives and pays off in much greater social harmony. Just walk the streets of Tokyo: few homeless sleeping on grates, no muggers lurking in the shadows."

42. See Wilson (1987).

43. Thomson (1992).

44. Folbre (1992).

45. New York Times (1992, p. C1).

46. Albany Times-Union (1995, p. A6). The Learning for Earning program was initiated in Georgia by U.S. House Speaker Newt Gingrich and subsequently implemented on a national scale. See also Tetzeli (1992, p. 80).

47. Kozol (1992, p. 277). See also Kozol's (1991) discussion of the state of American public education, and Bellah et al.'s (1991, p. 170) critique of the idea of an "education industry."

48. Hancock (1995, p. 44).

49. For a particularly insightful discussion of the penetration of market-based norms and metaphors into noneconomic realms of social life, see Schwartz (1994a, 1994b). Schwartz (1994b, p. 361) observes that "along with the language of the market, people have increasingly adopted the practices of the market." An example of the application of kin-based terminology to the marketplace, brought to our attention by an undergraduate student, is that of a "parent corporation."

50. Bellah et al. (1991, p. 291). Similar arguments about the consequences of economic "invasion" for other social

institutions can be found in Currie (1991), Schwartz (1994b), and Wolfe (1989).

51. See Snyder and Patterson (1987) for a discussion of research on parenting and juvenile delinquency.

52. Steffensmeier and Allan (1995). The overrepresentation of males is not always observed for minor forms of offending in self-report studies. When serious offenses are considered, however, the results of self-report studies are consistent with those based on other data sources.

53. Compared with males, female respondents in the 1993 General Social Survey reported spending more time with parents, siblings, and other relations (authors' calculations). See Thompson and Walker (1991) for a review of the literature on gender differences in family involvement.

54. The study of value orientations of high school students is reported in Beutel and Marini (1995). The quotation appears on p. 438. These authors also summarize research on gender differences in value orientations for adults. The reference to the greater emphasis on the goal of child bearing for females is based on the 1993 General Social Survey (authors' calculations).

55. Our explanation of gender differences in offending in the contemporary United States is consistent with observations for the mid–nineteenth century made by the classic social analyst, Alexis de Tocqueville. As Barry Schwartz (1994b, pp. 222–223) explains, de Tocqueville believed that women's extensive involvement in the family served as "the counterweight to the pursuit of selfish interests in the marketplace."

56. The reference to the "second shift" is from Hochschild (1989). Harris (1981, pp. 76–97) discusses declining commitment to family and parenting.

57. Gender convergence need not lead to an increase in crime rates. The logic of our argument implies that greater engagement of men in familial roles should reduce their exposure to anomic pressures and lower their criminal involvement to a level more similar to that of women, thereby reducing overall rates of crime. We discuss the importance for crime control of revitalizing the family in Chapter 5.

58. See Tonry (1995) for a summary of race differences in levels and patterns of criminal offending and an insightful discussion of the role of race in crime control policy and practice in the United States.

59. The term "urban plantation" is from Staples (1987). See Gutman (1976) for a compelling account of the efforts by black Americans after the Civil War to reunite families that had been split apart during slavery. Good discussions of the contemporary black family and the precarious position of inner-city families can be found in Cherlin (1992, pp. 91–123), Hacker (1992, pp. 67–92), and Wilson (1987).

60. See Massey and Denton (1993) for a penetrating treatment of racial segregation and the development of the ghetto underclass.

61. Jennifer Hochschild's *Facing Up to the American Dream* (1995) provides an exhaustive summary of survey research on blacks' and whites' perceptions and beliefs regarding the dominant success ideology. The quoted material in this paragraph is from pages 56–57 of Hochschild's book; see pages 72–88 for evidence on class differences in African Americans' attitudes toward the American Dream.

62. Nightingale (1993, pp. 148,160). Nightingale uses the term "commodity worship" to describe the acute consumption pressures experienced by some inner-city adolescents (see pp. 143ff).

5

Strengthening Social Institutions and Rethinking the American Dream

There is a hollowness at the core of a society if its members share no
common purpose, no mutual goals, no joint vision—nothing to believe in
except self-aggrandizement.

MARIAN WRIGHT EDELMAN[1]

In Dreams Begin Responsibilities

DELMORE SCHWARTZ[2]

In 1929, James Truslow Adams, historian of the American Dream, called attention to the alarming crime problem in the United States, but he never
pursued a rigorous analysis of the influence of the American Dream on
crime. Nonetheless, he believed that the task of reducing crime in America
was urgent and that it would require alterations in basic social and cultural
patterns. He also recognized the role of human agency in social change and
the importance of leadership at the highest levels in mobilizing the resources
necessary to reform the "very foundations" of American life. In his view, nothing less than American democracy itself was at stake. "We must rule or be
ruled," he wrote, because unless the crime problem is brought under control,
social order will sooner or later give way to chaos, opening the way for "the
dictator who inevitably 'saves society' when social insubordination and disinte-
gration have become intolerable."[3]

Adams directed his message for change, published in an essay on law obser-
vance, to Herbert Hoover. It is easy in retrospect to dismiss as futile his effort
to educate President Hoover on the nature of the crime problem. However,
Adams was well aware of the president's public policy limitations. Hoover may
not have understood the "magnitude and the causes of the danger which we

face," but at least he acknowledged that a crime problem existed. By contrast, his predecessor, Calvin Coolidge, "never troubled himself over the rising tide of crime and lawlessness, beyond seeing to it that Mrs. Coolidge was accompanied on her shopping by an armed protector."[4]

Several important lessons remain in Adams' attempts to educate the president and the public about crime. If Adams exaggerated the specter of social collapse and dictatorship, he recognized the genuine vulnerability of democratic rights and freedoms to demagogic appeals for "law and order." He also understood the importance of establishing a supportive intellectual climate for effective political leadership and public action. Hoover's moral appeals to citizens to do their "duty" by obeying the Eighteenth Amendment prohibition against the manufacture, sale, or transportation of intoxicating liquors were ineffective, in Adams' view, because they reflected a shallow appreciation of the American crime problem:

> The American problem, though complicated by Prohibition, lies far
> deeper; and it is the lack of understanding as to what the problem is that
> so greatly diminishes the force of Mr. Hoover's appeal to us as citizens
> anxious to do our duty toward society.[5]

Adams also contributes very important insights regarding the causes of crime and prospects for crime policy in America. His message is organized around two themes that are central to our arguments. First, the roots of the American crime problem lie deep within our cultural and institutional history. "Lawlessness," by which Adams meant a generalized disrespect for law as such, is part of the American heritage. Prohibition may have contributed to the problem, he wrote in a 1928 article published in the *Atlantic* entitled "Our Lawless Heritage,"

> but it is operating upon a population already the most lawless in spirit of
> any in the great modern civilized countries. Lawlessness has been and is
> one of the most distinctive American traits. . . . It is needless to say that we
> are not going to be able to shed this heritage quickly or easily.[6]

Second, because high rates of crime are neither recent nor ephemeral characteristics of American society, responses to crime must be equally fundamental if they are to be effective. According to Adams, the "spirit" of lawlessness, which is very similar to what we have termed the ethic of anomie, will give way only when the preconditions for respect for law have been established. These include knowledge of the nature and limits of law on the part of lawmakers and the public, and the impartial application of legal sanctions against "millionaires" and "highly placed officials in Washington," as well as against the "ordinary criminal." Most important, the American spirit of lawlessness will not abate "until the ideal of quickly accumulated wealth, by any means whatever, is made subordinate to the ideal of private and public virtue."[7]

Adams does not describe in detail how these changes are to come about, in particular how virtue would overcome the goal of material accumulation, except to propose that the president has, if he would only seize it, an opportunity to exercise essential moral leadership. Although directed at Herbert Hoover in 1929, Adams' call for moral "regeneration" continues to be relevant to present-day political and cultural conditions, as the quotation from Marian Wright Edelman at the beginning of this chapter suggests. If the president, in Adams' words,

> will undertake to show the people what underlies their problem, and assume the leadership in a crusade to reform the very foundations of their life, . . . then he will prove the leader for whom America waits, and patriotism and nobility may again rise above efficiency and wealth. By that path only can America regain respect for law and for herself. . . . America can be saved, but it must be by regeneration, not by efficiency.[8]

We share Adams' belief that significant reductions in crime in the United States will require fundamental changes in the social and cultural order. If our diagnosis of the problem is correct—if high levels of crime derive from the very organization of American society—the logical solution is social reorganization. This will entail, in our view, both institutional reform and cultural regeneration. Before sketching the kinds of institutional and cultural changes that might reduce crime rates, however, it is important first to consider conventional approaches to crime control and their limitations.

CONVENTIONAL STRATEGIES FOR CRIME CONTROL

The point of departure for this discussion is current policy, and proposals for alternative policies, championed by what we will call the "conservative" and "liberal" political camps. Current policy, informed largely by conservative views, has not stemmed the tide of high levels of serious crime in the United States. However, proposals from the liberal camp to complement conservative "get tough" strategies with social reforms to expand opportunities for those "locked out" of the American Dream have not been any more successful in reducing levels of serious crime. The reason for these failures, we suggest, is that both conservative and liberal strategies reinforce the very qualities of American culture that lead to high rates of crime in the first place.

The Conservative Camp: The War on Crime

Conservative crime control policies are draped explicitly in the metaphors of war. We have declared war on crime, and on drugs, which are presumed to promote crime. Criminals, according to this view, have taken the streets, blocks, and sometimes entire neighborhoods from law-abiding citizens. The function of crime control policy is to recapture the streets from criminals to make them safe for the rest of us. This is accomplished by a range of initiatives encompassing law enforcement, criminal prosecution, court decisions, and sanctions policy.

Let us summarize briefly the conservative scenario. The police will act swiftly to remove criminals from the streets, prosecutors will vigorously bring their cases to court without plea-bargaining them to charges carrying lesser penalties, judges and juries will have less discretion in determining the penalties imposed (for example, "three strikes" laws that mandate extended prison sentences for three-time offenders), and more criminals will serve longer sentences for their crimes. Corrections officials will thus keep offenders in prison for longer periods of time, both because offenders are serving longer sentences and because officials will have less discretion in granting parole to offenders. The cumulative effects of these "get tough" actions will be lower crime rates brought about by increases both in the deterrent effects of punishment and in what criminologists term the "incapacitation effects" of imprisonment. With respect to deterrence, stiffer penalties will raise the costs of crime, thereby dissuading potential offenders from committing their first crimes and convincing previous offenders that it is too costly to repeat their misdeeds. The simple logic of incapacitation is that offenders who are in prison will be unable to commit crimes against the innocent public.

Conservatives have been successful in influencing crime control policies over the course of recent decades. For the twenty-four-year period between 1968 and 1992, the White House was occupied for all but four years by Republican presidents who proudly proclaimed their credentials as "law and order" advocates. Republican control over the presidency resulted in the nomination of conservative justices to the Supreme Court and conservative judges to the federal judiciary, and it facilitated legislative changes consistent with the conservative agenda on crime control. Among the most important of these changes was the widespread adoption during the 1980s of mandatory-minimum sentencing laws.

Mandatory-Minimum Sentencing and the Drug War Mandatory-minimum laws specify the minimum sentence for crimes and, in principle, prohibit courts and correctional agencies from modifying them. The intent of such sentencing policy is to increase both the certainty and the severity of punishment for persons convicted of the most serious crimes. Mandatory-minimum sentencing has been applied with special force to drug trafficking, resulting in extraordinary increases in the incarceration rates of drug offenders. Data from the National Corrections Reporting Program (NCRP) indicate that over half (52 percent) of the increase in prison admissions during the 1980s were for drug offenses. According to a leading criminal justice policy analyst, the use of mandatory-minimum sentencing in the war on drugs has "elevated the severity of punishment for drug sales to a level comparable to that for homicide."[9]

By any reasonable standard, the policies associated with the war on crime and drugs have been a dismal failure. Rates of serious crime in America have fluctuated over time, sometimes increasing and sometimes decreasing, but they have remained at very high levels despite the implementation of a host of conservative policies. Moreover, Americans do not perceive themselves to be safer than in the past. If anything, as we documented in Chapter 2, fear of crime and preoccupation with personal safety have intensified over the past twenty-five years.

The Expansion of Punitive Social Control The war on crime has achieved one noteworthy victory, suggested in our discussion of mandatory-minimum sentencing, although it is surely a pyrrhic one: incarceration levels have soared. The number of persons sentenced to more than one year in state and federal prisons surpassed the one million mark in 1994. There were 1,012,463 sentenced prisoners in 1994, a rate of 387 prisoners per 100,000 population. In 1980, by contrast, 315,974 persons were serving time in state and federal prisons, a rate of 139 per 100,000 population.[10] The rapid escalation of incarceration has produced a costly and potentially very dangerous "capacity crisis" in the correctional system. As incarceration rates increased throughout the 1970s and 1980s, national attention began to focus on the problem of overcrowding in prisons and jails. By the end of 1994, state prisons were operating with inmate populations that averaged 117 percent of their "highest" capacity, which is the capacity level required to maintain basic custody, security, and custodial operations, limited programming, and little else. The federal system operated at 125 percent of inmate capacity. The American Correctional Association, meanwhile, recommends that a prison never run at greater than 90 percent of capacity, to allow for administrative flexibility and response to emergencies. Only three states met this "industry standard" in 1994, and thirty-seven states operated above 100 percent of "highest" capacity. The situation in local jails is no better, in part because thousands of state prisoners are held in local jails because of crowding in state facilities.[11]

The extraordinary increase in the population of prisons and jails is only part of a larger expansion of formal, punitive social control in the United States. As of the end of 1993, 4.9 million Americans, 2.6 percent of all adults, were under some form of correctional sanction. Roughly 1.4 million were in prison or jail, and the remaining 3.5 million were under supervision in the community (about 2.8 million on probation and 0.7 million on parole).[12] Between 1980 and 1993, the number of adults under some form of correctional sanction in the United States increased by 165 percent. At present rates of growth, 6 percent of the adult population will be subject to some form of correctional supervision by the year 2000, and 10 percent of American adults will be under correctional control by 2006.[13]

As noted in Chapter 1, African Americans currently are subject to levels of punitive social control that are much higher than these projected estimates for the population as a whole. African Americans have been hit hard by the war against crime—and especially by the war against drugs. In his 1992 presidential address to the American Society of Criminology, Alfred Blumstein characterized rising levels of arrest and incarceration of black Americans as nothing less than

> a major assault on the black community. One can be reasonably confident
> that if a similar assault was affecting the white community, there would be

a strong and effective effort to change either the laws or the enforcement policy.[14]

Whether or not black Americans have been targeted explicitly, disturbing parallels exist between the massive expansion in formal social control during the 1980s and the infamous "Black Codes" of the post–Civil War South. Most of the southern states passed such vagrancy laws, allowing for the arrest of unemployed and "idle" blacks.[15] However, the aggressive sanctions policies of recent years have not resulted in declines in offending among blacks. On the contrary, rates of violent crime and drug offending among young blacks increased sharply during the last half of the 1980s and early 1990s.[16]

Unintended Consequences of Expanded Punitive Control Not only has the extension of the reach of the criminal justice system failed to reduce crime; it also tends to undermine the capacity of the system to realize an equally important objective: justice. Excessive caseloads put pressure on the major participants in the adjudication process—district attorneys, defense lawyers (especially public defenders), and judges—to dispense with cases quickly. The result is a preoccupation with efficiency rather than with the rights of criminal defendants.[17] A concern with the simple management of large numbers of cases also pervades the correctional system. Indeed, criminologists Malcolm Feeley and Jonathan Simon have argued that a new way of perceiving the very functions of criminal sanctions has become dominant in criminology and criminal justice. According to this "new penology," the focus of corrections has shifted away from a concern with administering levels of punishment that individuals deserve, or a concern with rehabilitating these offenders, to a preoccupation with more efficient "risk management" of dangerous populations.[18]

The unfortunate and unintended consequences of the war on crime, however, extend far beyond the criminal justice system itself. Crackdowns on crime are directed at those populations considered to be most dangerous to society. This implies that minority groups will be affected disproportionately by these efforts. As we have seen, this has been precisely the case for black Americans, many of whom quite understandably resent the differential treatment imposed on them by vigorous law enforcement efforts. It should come as little surprise, therefore, that police-citizen confrontations involving minority group members are likely to be filled with tension and hostility and that they can ignite episodes of collective disorder.

In addition, given the greater criminal involvement of males in comparison with females, and of young males in particular, extremely high levels of incarceration can have devastating implications for the sex ratio of a community and, in turn, for family relations. The large-scale removal of young males from the general population depletes the supply of potential marriage partners for young females. In so doing, expansive incarceration policies impede the formation of traditional families and thereby encourage, indirectly, higher rates of female-headed households and illegitimacy—precisely the types of family conditions that have been linked with high rates of crime.[19] In short, the war on crime has not only failed to realize the goal of significant crime reduction; it has exacerbated the very problem that it is supposed to solve.

The failure of conservative crime control policies reflects the warfare mentality that provides their justification. This is why it is so politically dangerous to call for an end to current policy, even for those who are willing to acknowledge its limitations. It appears defeatist to advocate limits on the costs of criminal sanctions, or on the proportion of the population it is reasonable or desirable to place under correctional control, when crime control is imbued with the metaphors of war. A former official in the current drug war is said to have compared the underlying logic of the campaign with Humpty Dumpty:

> When all the King's horses and all the King's men couldn't put Humpty together again, the response was merely to double the number of horses and men, rather than to recognize at some point the futility of the effort.[20]

However, reports of violent conflict from the "battle zones" of American cities suggest that the war on crime is more than just a rhetorical device: it is a classic instance of the sociological self-fulfilling prophesy. It begins with a definition of the situation that likens the crime problem to war. The war on crime, in turn, reinforces the cultural and social arrangements that produce warlike conditions in the society. The response is to intensify the war on crime. An alternative response would be to change the initial definition of crime as war and criminals as "enemies." This is the approach to crime control taken by the liberal camp, although it too ends up reproducing social and cultural conditions conducive to crime.

The Liberal Camp: The War on Poverty and on Inequality of Opportunity

In contrast to conservative crackdowns on criminals, the liberal approach to crime control emphasizes correctional policies and broader social reforms intended to expand opportunities for those "locked out" of the American Dream. This approach is based on the premise that the poor and disadvantaged want to conform to the law and that they commit crimes only when doing so is necessary to achieve goals that cannot be achieved through conformity. The temptations for crime can thus be lessened by providing access to the legitimate means of success for those who lack opportunities. For those who have already become enmeshed in the criminal justice system, liberals call for rehabilitation and reform, with a heavy emphasis on training and skill development to allow offenders to compete more effectively for jobs upon reentry into society.

Liberals, like conservatives, have enjoyed some notable successes in getting their policies implemented. A good example of liberal strategies for general social reform is provided by the War on Poverty during the 1960s. Many of the programs associated with this initiative were justified with explicit reference to crime reduction. Perhaps the most famous of these was the Mobilization for Youth program, which sought to reduce crime and delinquency in a depressed area of Manhattan by expanding educational and employment opportunities. This program was organized in part by Richard Cloward, one of the leading figures associated with the anomie perspective on crime and delinquency.[21]

Effects of Liberal Policies on Crime Rates Little evidence suggests that the liberal strategies, including the Mobilization for Youth program, have been any more effective than the conservative approaches in reducing levels of crime.[22] Crime rates increased markedly during the height of liberal social reform in the 1960s and early 1970s. Some liberal advocates have argued that their approach was never really tried, that the War on Poverty was underfunded, that it was more image than reality, or that it was quickly overwhelmed by other issues, such as the Vietnam War. Typical of this view is Ruth Sidel's comment:

> The War on Poverty was woefully inadequate to reverse the damage that was done, particularly to blacks, in our society; and no sooner did it get started than Vietnam, inflation, and the Nixon administration had begun to subvert it.[23]

However, the fact is that poverty rates in the United States did decline during the 1960s and most of the 1970s. Unless official poverty rates are rejected as grossly invalid indicators of impediments to economic opportunity, then, based on the liberal view, some relief from serious crime should have coincided with the realization of genuine social reform.[24]

We may question the effectiveness of the liberal approach to crime control for additional reasons. First, it is difficult to see how the liberal explanation of crime and the policies based on it would apply to the crimes committed by persons at the top of the opportunity structure, crimes that are far from rare and that are very costly to society. Second, although certain forms of serious crime are disproportionately committed by the poor, crime rates do not rise and fall in a direct way with poverty rates, unemployment rates, or other indicators of economic deprivation. In fact, the opposite is the case for certain historical periods.

Crime rates fell during the Great Depression of the 1930s and rose dramatically during the prosperous 1960s. Crime rates declined during the mid-1970s and then again during the early 1980s, but in both instances the reductions coincided with periods of economic recession. A full assessment of changes in levels of serious crime must, of course, encompass a wide range of causal factors in addition to economic opportunities, such as changes in the age composition of the population and in the routine activities that make people and property more or less vulnerable or attractive targets for crime.[25] Even so, the evidence fails to support the proposition that reductions in crime follow in any simple, direct manner from an expansion of economic opportunities.

The failure of the liberal approach to crime control, we suggest, is due to an incomplete understanding of the social sources of crime in American society. Liberals are aware of the feeble institutional infrastructures to be found in many impoverished communities and neighborhoods, and they recognize the devastating implications of such structural conditions for efforts at crime control. However, liberals ignore cultural pressures for crime that emanate from the American Dream itself, from its celebration of the unrestrained, competitive pursuit of monetary success. Greater equality of opportunity and a redistribution of economic resources would not by themselves diminish the importance of winning and losing, nor would they eliminate the strong temptations to try to win by any means necessary.

Unintended Consequences of Liberal Reform Not only do liberal crime control strategies fail to target the full range of social causes of high crime rates in the United States, but, like conservative strategies, they are self-defeating when enacted in the absence of more fundamental social change. Policies that reduce discriminatory barriers to occupational achievement and broaden access to education, to the extent that they are successful, promote social mobility and extend the reach of the American Dream to persons and groups who have historically been excluded from its benefits. This is, of course, the very point of much liberal social policy. But, in so doing, these policies reinforce the commitment to the American Dream itself and hence sustain its criminogenic consequences. A population would not long remain wedded to the idea that everyone should struggle relentlessly to get ahead if hardly anyone actually ever did get ahead.[26]

In addition, the social mobility fostered by liberal social reform may aggravate the crime problem in another way, as suggested by the sociologist William Julius Wilson. Wilson describes the process through which poverty, crime, and other social problems become concentrated in urban neighborhoods. When better-off residents depart for other areas of the city or the suburbs, they take with them skills, resources, and models of conventional behavior that contribute to community stability. They leave behind, all else equal, a community that is less able to exercise informal social control over its members, less able to protect itself from outsiders, and therefore more vulnerable to crime. As crime rates rise, more residents depart, again those with the best prospects being the first to go. The concentration of economic and social disadvantage increases, and crime rates continue to climb.[27]

Wilson's analysis of neighborhood transition draws heavily on the social disorganization tradition associated with the Chicago school in urban sociology; in fact, he illustrates his argument with data from Chicago community areas. Writing in the 1980s, however, Wilson supplements his analysis with an account of the growth in mobility opportunities for middle- and working-class blacks that accompanied declines in discriminatory barriers in education and work, and, to a more limited degree, housing during the previous two decades. The opening of the opportunity structure enabled many, though far from all, blacks to join the urban exodus of the previous thirty years. Even blacks who did not leave the central city because of continuing residential discrimination in suburban areas were able in greater numbers than ever before to move away from "declining" neighborhoods. As whites had been able to do for decades, blacks could now abandon old and deteriorating neighborhoods for new, more stable ones. They could participate in the American tradition of linking geographic and social mobility. Now, like other Americans, when they moved up, they could move out. As a result, unintentional to be sure, expansions in opportunities for some black Americans led to expansions in crime rates for others.

We do not mean to exaggerate either the effects on neighborhood crime rates of the outmigration of better-off residents or, for that matter, the number of black Americans who have benefited from equal opportunity policies. Nor do we condone in any way the racial discrimination that "kept blacks in their place" in earlier periods. Further, it would be absurd to blame those individuals, of whatever race, who flee crime-ridden communities in search of greater personal security. Their decisions and actions are understandable and, from the individual point of view, entirely justifiable.

We also do not mean to belittle the achievements of liberal social reform. The expansion of opportunities produces a broad range of benefits regardless of any impact on crime rates; there is more to improving the quality of life in a society than reducing the risks of criminal victimization. Providing everyone with the maximum feasible degree of opportunity for the realization of human potential is a worthy cultural goal as a matter of simple justice. Our point is simply that a war on poverty or on inequality of opportunity is not likely to be an effective strategy for crime control in the absence of other cultural and structural changes.

Beyond Liberalism and Conservatism

The failure of both liberals and conservatives to offer effective solutions to the crime problem ultimately reflects the inability, or unwillingness, of advocates of either approach to question the fundamental features of American society. In a sense, both are prisoners of the dominant culture. Conservatives and liberals alike embrace the American Dream without reservation and search for an external "enemy" with which to engage in a war. Conservatives direct the war against the "wicked" persons who are held to represent a danger to society.[28] The enemies for liberals are not bad persons but bad social conditions, imperfections of the social structure that make it difficult or impossible for some people to conform to dominant norms. These social imperfections, including poverty, racial discrimination, and lack of education, are typically viewed by liberals as a betrayal of the American Dream. Neither group entertains the possibility that the enemy comes from within, that the causes of crime lie within the dominant culture itself.

As a consequence of this intellectual blind spot, the policies of both conservatives and liberals are severely constrained by the logic of the existing culture and, in ironic ways, reflect this logic. The conservative approach promotes crime control policies without limits and at any cost. This expansive and expensive strategy for controlling crime embodies the anomic quality of American culture: the cultural imperative to pursue goals by any means necessary.

Liberal policies, in contrast, strengthen the other element of American culture that is criminogenic—the excessive emphasis on the competitive, individualistic struggle for monetary success. Liberals propose, in effect, that strengthening the American Dream will solve the problems caused by the American Dream. In short, both liberal and conservative policies for crime control are ultimately self-defeating because they reproduce the very cultural and social conditions that generate the distinctively high levels of crime for which the United States is known throughout the world.

Any significant reduction in crime will require moving beyond the failed ideas and policies associated with both ends of the conventional political spectrum. However, the policies that we suggest are also not likely to bring about substantial reductions in crime in the short run. We are not aware of any policy solutions for the crime problem that could have this effect. This is not simply because past and present policies have been hamstrung by the liberal and conservative alternatives; it is also because the conditions that lead to crime cannot be ameliorated by "policy" as such, or at least by policy that is politically feasible. In the United States, substantial crime reductions require *social change*, not simply new social policy. Policy, on the other hand, is most often concerned with making existing arrangements more *efficient*. The function of policy is to improve existing means of achieving collective goals; rarely does policy seek to alter the goals themselves. As one analyst suggests, addressing the "basic causes" of a problem may be of little interest to policy makers because they are under strong political pressures to define problems in terms of available solutions, and they typically lack the material or political resources to alter basic causes.[29]

Genuine crime control requires transformation from within, a reorganization of social institutions and a regeneration of cultural commitments. This is certainly a formidable task given the powerful influence of existing cultural beliefs and structural arrangements. The task is not, however, an impossible one. Culture and social structure inevitably place constraints on human action, but these constraints are of a unique type. Unlike the limits imposed by the natural world, the social world is ultimately created and re-created by the participants themselves.

Sociologist Peter Berger uses the metaphor of a puppet to describe the paradox of constraint and potentiality in human action.[30] He compares the expectations and requirements of social roles to the strings that regulate the movements of a puppet. The puppet's movements are, of course, constrained by the strings. At the same time, Berger cautions that the puppet metaphor should not be stretched too far. Human beings are not mindless puppets. Each of us individually is able to look up and examine the mechanism from which the strings hang, and, collectively, we can redesign the mechanism. Human actors, in other words, have the capacity to become aware of the social constraints on action and to change these constraints. In the next section, we sketch the kinds of changes in the institutional and cultural "mechanism" of American society that offer some promise of meaningful reductions in levels of serious crime.

CRIME REDUCTION THROUGH SOCIAL REORGANIZATION

Our prescriptions for crime reduction follow logically from our analysis of the causes of high levels of crime. To recapitulate very briefly: We contend that criminal activity is stimulated by strong cultural pressures for monetary success combined with anomie, a normative order with weak restraints on the selection of the means to pursue success. This anomic cultural condition is accompanied by an institutional balance of power in which the economy assumes dominance over other social institutions. Economic dominance diminishes the attractiveness of alternatives to the goal of monetary success and impedes the capacity of other institutions to perform their distinctive functions, including social control. High levels of crime thus reflect intrinsic elements of American culture and the corrosive impact of these cultural elements on social structure.

It follows from this analysis, moving back up the causal chain from high levels of crime through social structure and culture, that crime reductions would result from policies that strengthen social structure and weaken the criminogenic qualities of American culture. More specifically, crime reductions would follow from policies and social changes that vitalize families, schools, and the political system, thereby enhancing the "drawing power" of the distinctive goals associated with these institutions and strengthening their capacity to exercise social control. This institutional vitalization would, in turn, temper the anomic qualities and the intense pressures for monetary success associated with the American Dream. Finally, cultural regeneration—modifications in the American Dream itself—would promote and sustain institutional change and reduce cultural pressures for crime. We begin our discussion of social reorganization with a consideration of the structural dimension: institutional reform.

Institutional Reform

The Family and Schools Initiatives such as the provision of family leave, job sharing for husbands and wives, flexible work schedules, employer-provided child care, and a host of other "pro-family" economic policies should help alter the balance between the economic demands faced by parents and their obligations and opportunities to devote more time and energy to exclusively family concerns. In many families, parents and children spend very little time with each other. In a 1990 survey of American students in the sixth through the twelfth grades, half of the high school students reported that they did not share evening meals with their parents on a daily basis, and nearly half of the sixth graders reported that they spent two or more hours a day at home without an adult present.[31]

Policies that enable parents to spend more time with their children should not only strengthen family controls over children's behavior but also enable the schools to carry out their control functions more effectively. Teachers and educational researchers alike maintain that the absence of parental support for education handicaps the schools in their efforts to motivate learning and keep children engaged in the educational process. Yet only about half of the ninth- and twelfth-graders in the survey cited here reported that their parents "talk with me about school." Only one-third reported that their parents attended school meetings or events.

These examples illustrate the point made in Chapter 4 concerning the interdependent nature of social institutions. The capacity of any institution to fulfill its distinctive function is dependent on the effective functioning of the others. Not surprisingly, then, the lack of articulation between the family and the schools has unfortunate consequences for society at large. As one educational researcher observes, the poor articulation between the home and the school reflects and reinforces a "serious erosion of social capital" in American communities. If children do not see adults often, if their relationships with adults are "fleeting," adults cannot serve as effective deterrents and as positive influences on children's behavior. The social bonds necessary for discipline, emanating from both the family and the schools, are weakened as a result.[32]

Policies aimed at strengthening the schools must proceed in concert with those designed to improve family functioning. These policies must confront two interrelated problems: (1) strengthening external controls and (2) strengthening the engagement of people—parents and teachers, as well as children and students—in the distinctive goals and "logics" of these institutions. It is worth pondering the mixed messages that our society currently sends regarding the best way to repair and strengthen families and schools.

The message regarding families is to avoid having one as long as possible. It is difficult to think of a single source of cultural encouragement in the United States today for young people to get married and to have children—in either order. In the current obsession with out-of-wedlock births, it is scarcely noticed that birth rates among young women have declined sharply since 1960. The proportion of births to unmarried women has risen, but this is because marriage rates have fallen even faster than birth rates. Over 80 percent of males and more than 66 percent of females between the ages of twenty and twenty-four were single (that is, never married) in 1993, compared with 55 percent of males and 36 percent of females in this age group in 1970. Over the same period, the percentage of males in their late twenties who were single grew from 19 to 48 percent. Over 30 percent of males in their early thirties were single in 1993, compared with less than 10 percent two decades earlier. Although in each age group females were more likely than males to be married, the fraction remaining single grew just as rapidly.[33]

The apparent decline in the attractiveness of marriage in the United States is a cause for some concern given the central role that marriage plays in creating what anthropologist David Murray refers to as "bridges of social connectedness." Marriages give rise to reciprocal obligations that bind not only the spouses themselves but other family members and friends on both sides. This in turn promotes "moral feelings of attachment and integration" that help hold a society and culture together. In Murray's words, "individual marriages are the rivets of the social order, local-level attachments by which the whole structure is ultimately assembled."[34]

Yet the loud message to young people is to stop having children rather than to start forming families. Whatever the salutary effects of this message, it serves to reinforce the view of families as burdens to be shouldered only after a long period of economic preparation. We do not necessarily advocate early marriage as a form of crime control, but it seems that a society with a professed commitment to "family values" should provide more cultural and social support for family formation. As a practical matter, this support will require lessening the dependence of marital and family decision making on purely economic considerations.

With respect to schools, a popular message of the 1990s sounds the market-oriented theme of "choice": Bad schools will be driven out of business by good ones if obstacles blocking open markets in schooling are eliminated. This will occur if people are given the options of purchasing their educations in either public or private schools and of enrolling in schools outside of specific attendance areas or districts. Again, although such proposals may have particular merits, their general effect is to reinforce the market mentality of American education.[35] One can scarcely blame students for asking whether this or that aspect of their education "pays" when this is exactly the question that dominates current educational policy discussion.

A rather different type of policy for schools is suggested by our argument. Schools should be enabled to devote themselves to their distinctive goal of formal learning. This requires, as we have suggested, stronger parental support for the educational function. However, it also requires that children's economic prospects become tied less closely to their performance in school.

Those who look back fondly to the "good old days" of strict discipline and respect for learning that are supposed to have once characterized the American public school system often forget that one reason the schools could educate more effectively in the past is because they did not have to educate as universally. In a world where labor markets offered jobs that did not require a high school education, the public schools operated much more selectively than they do now. Students who flunked out or who were expelled for disciplinary reasons, or who left because they simply did not like school, did not as a rule end up in the streets; they went to work, they formed families, or they joined the military.

Not long ago, Americans depended less on schools for economic rewards. As recently as 1960, only 43 percent of whites and 20 percent of blacks age 25 and older had completed four or more years of high school. By 1993, 81 percent of whites and 70 percent of blacks in this age group had completed high school.[36] In a society where "good jobs" require a college degree or some other form of training beyond high school, and where military service requires a high school diploma, schools will daily confront students who, at best, calculate their "investment" in education according to future earnings. At worst, they will find themselves in chronic conflicts with students made hopeless by the knowledge that proper educational certification is a necessary—but far from sufficient—condition for economic success.

The Polity Turning to the institution of the polity, our analysis points to two types of policy shifts: (1) reform of the formal system of crime control, particularly the correctional system, and (2) the creation of broader patterns of social participation and social control beyond the criminal justice system.

Correctional policy that is consistent with our analysis of the crime problem begins with a fundamental question that neither the liberal nor the conservative camp addresses: What is the optimum proportion of the population that should be under the jurisdiction of correctional agencies?[37] One may be tempted to answer zero to this question, but unless we are willing to assume a crime rate of zero or are willing to let all convicted offenders go unpunished, some proportion of the population must be under some form of correctional control at all times. So, again, what is the optimum proportion?

This is not a "policy question" narrowly defined; it is a question designed to stimulate a different way of thinking about crime control policy. It is a political question, and it most certainly is a moral question, because it requires judgments about the goals of crime control and not simply choices among more efficient or less efficient means to achieve a predefined goal, or, as in current policy, among several ill-defined and conflicting goals.[38] A central goal of any approach to crime control that is based on our analysis is to reduce cultural support for crime. A prerequisite for accomplishing this objective is to end the war on crime. We are not proposing, of course, to end efforts at crime control. On the contrary, we believe that effective crime control can begin only when control is gained over current crime policy. Achieving control of crime policy requires placing limits on the costs of crime control, especially the costs of corrections. Although cost containment will not be easy, it is essential if the anomic and perverse consequences of the war on crime are to be halted.

The idea of *intermediate sanctions*, which are community-based punishments situated between ordinary probation and prison, has been promoted by correctional reformers as a way to reduce the costs and crowding of correctional supervision while maintaining a high level of public safety. Sentencing policy based on the principle of intermediate sanctions would impose the kinds of limits on crime control that are consistent with our analysis. We question, however, whether the intensified supervision associated with most intermediate sanctions will produce the cost savings claimed by some advocates.[39]

A key issue is whether the flow of offenders into the new community programs consists primarily of those who would have gone to prison or those who would have been placed on ordinary probation. If intermediate sanctions programs draw primarily from the pool of prison-bound offenders, they can help lower correctional costs and relieve overcrowding in correctional facilities. However, the great majority of persons serving time in prison have been convicted of violent crimes, have committed violent crimes in the past, or are repeat felony offenders.[40] These offenders are not likely to be deemed suitable candidates for community-based programs, no matter how intensive the supervision. If, on the other hand, offenders who would otherwise have received ordinary probation are the main recipients of intermediate sanctions, then the cost savings of these intermediate punishments are greatly reduced to pay for heightened supervision of offenders in the community.

The net impact of intermediate sanctions is, then, difficult to discern. Interestingly, however, this is one of their great advantages over current policy. Reconciling tough choices regarding cost, safety, and justice presupposes some agreement over the priorities of the criminal justice system. Current policy is politically pleasing because it does not require consensus building or difficult trade-offs among competing values and interests; there are no limits in a war on crime. The system we prefer does not have this spurious benefit because, by introducing a measure of restraint into crime control policy, it would make explicit both the scope and the purposes of punishment.

Reforms that are limited to the criminal justice system, however, will not by themselves produce appreciable reductions in crime. Broader changes within the polity are necessary to nurture the sense of collective obligation and individual duty essential for the effective functioning of formal social controls. One proposal that appears especially promising in this respect is the creation of a national service corps. If it is to contribute to crime control, such a system must be universalistic and involve an array of opportunities and obligations to serve local communities and the society as a whole. It can perform a particularly important integrative function by providing education, training in needed skills, and meaningful social controls for adolescents and young adults who have graduated from or dropped out of school, have not found work that will lead to a career, and who have outgrown the reach of their parents but have not yet formed families of their own. In short, by offering an institutional mooring for young people during the transition to adulthood, national service promises to bolster social control and facilitate "maturational reform," that is, the process through which young people involved in common forms of delinquency turn away from illegal behavior as they mature and assume adult obligations.

A specific form of national service with direct relevance to crime control policy is a Police Corps of young people trained as police officers who would serve on local forces for periods of two to four years. The concept was endorsed by President Bill Clinton in the early 1990s as part of his proposal to provide college assistance in return for community service. One commentator advocated the Police Corps as the basis for President Clinton's efforts to build support for his broader philosophy of national service: "It's the logical place to start now, as the new President embarks on his most ambitious goal—to rebuild a national sense of community, responsibility, and public altruism."[41]

Although the Police Corps was not implemented, President Clinton was able to establish the Corporation for National and Community Service, better known as "AmeriCorps." AmeriCorps is a voluntary program of community service with strong crime prevention and public safety objectives. The program is open to persons of all ages; however, most volunteers are young adults who receive a living allowance and money toward college in return for their one or two years of service. Given its modest size (it was funded at $215 million in 1995) and voluntary nature, AmeriCorps does not significantly alter the level or quality of social participation by young people in the United States. Nevertheless, it serves as a prototype for the kind of political reform that, by actively engaging the young in community service, strengthens the sense of collective goal attainment that is the central and distinguishing function of the polity.[42]

Social Stratification and the Economy Finally, our analysis has important implications for the system of social stratification and the interrelations between this system and the economy. The relationship between stratification and crime has been the focus of extensive research and theorizing in modern criminology. Conventional approaches to the stratification–crime relationship, however, direct attention almost exclusively to a single feature of the stratification system: the distribution of opportunities for economic rewards. These explanations typically attribute crime to inequality in economic opportunities. We have maintained that greater equality of opportunity is not likely to eliminate pressures to succeed at any cost. The mere existence of unequal *outcomes* is likely to generate such pressures, regardless of the openness of the stratification system, if monetary success reigns supreme as a cultural goal and the economy dominates the institutional structure of society.

It might seem on the surface that the solution to the crime problem lies in greater equality of outcomes. However, it is not merely the shape of the distribution of material and symbolic rewards in America that contributes to crime but rather the mechanism by which rewards are distributed. In this respect, our analysis is informed by Marx's insight that the distribution of the means of consumption is ultimately dependent on the "conditions of production themselves."[43] The conditions of production in American society dictate that the distribution of rewards be tied to economic functions: either the performance of occupational roles or the possession of capital. In other words, the wealth that is produced within the economy is also distributed almost exclusively in accordance with economic criteria by labor and capital markets. To shore up such other institutions as the family, schools, and the polity relative to the economy, a greater share of the national wealth will have to be allocated on the basis of noneconomic criteria.

We are not endorsing the nationalization of the means of production to rebalance institutions. The political and economic failures of state socialist societies have been made glaringly apparent by recent history. Rather, the model that appears promising is that of the mixed economies in Europe and Japan. These nations have implemented a wide range of social policies and programs to ensure that material well-being is not strictly tied to economic functions and to guarantee that noneconomic roles receive meaningful financial support from collective resources.

Evidence suggests, moreover, that governmental efforts to "tame the market" by providing guarantees of minimal levels of material well-being are associated with comparatively low levels of serious crime. Figure 5–1 depicts

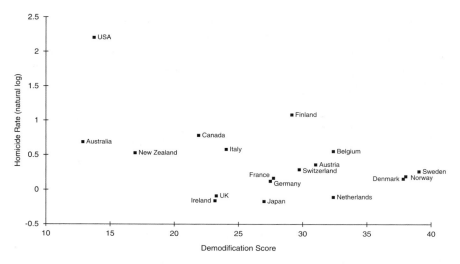

FIGURE 5–1 Scatterplot of Homicide Rates and Decommodification Scores for Esping-Andersen's Eighteen-Nation Sample

the relationship between the average homicide rate over the 1980–90 period and a measure of the extensiveness and generosity of social welfare policies for a sample of eighteen advanced capitalist nations. The welfare measure—referred to as the "decommodification index"—was created by the political scientist Gosta Esping-Andersen. The index reflects the ease of access to welfare entitlements, their income replacement value, and the range of social statuses and conditions that they cover. High scores on this index indicate comprehensive and unrestrictive welfare policies, whereas low scores indicate welfare systems characterized by relatively low benefit levels and strict eligibility requirements.

The relationship revealed in Figure 5–1, although not a perfect linear one, is consistent with our theoretical explanation of societal levels of crime.[44] Capitalist nations that limit dependence on the market for material well-being, as reflected in high decommodification scores, tend to exhibit comparatively low homicide rates. In contrast, nations in which citizens are highly dependent on market outcomes for their basic survival tend to have comparatively high homicide rates, with the United States serving as a striking case in point. The mechanism through which material rewards are distributed in capitalist societies—specifically, the extent to which market forces are moderated and counterbalanced by the welfare state—thus appears to be related to overall levels of the most serious of crimes, criminal homicide.[45]

To summarize: the structural changes that could lead to significant reductions in crime are those that promote a rebalancing of social institutions. These changes would involve reducing the subordination to the economy of the family, schools, the polity, and the general system of social stratification. Most of the specific proposals for institutional change that we have put forth are not particularly novel. They have been advanced by others in different contexts and with different agendas. These proposals, however, typically are considered in isolation from one another. For example, conservatives who bemoan the demise of the family and call for its rejuvenation rarely pursue the logical implications of their analyses and proposals. They fail to recognize or acknowledge that the vitalization of the family requires changes in the economy that are likely to be very distasteful to conservatives on ideological grounds.

The distinctive and powerful feature of the sociological paradigm is that it directs attention to the interconnections among social institutions. Because of these interconnections, piecemeal reforms are likely to be ineffective. Moreover, our analytical framework implies that institutional reforms must go hand in hand with cultural change because culture and institutional structures are themselves inextricably bound. It is to the matter of cultural change that we now turn.

The Task of Cultural Regeneration

A basic premise of this book is that the beliefs, values, and goals associated with the American Dream are firmly entrenched in the American historical experience and consciousness. If this premise is correct, it would be fanciful to entertain the possibility of any wholesale rejection of the American Dream.[46] Such a radical cultural transformation is not required, however, to begin the process of enriching noneconomic institutions. Instead, by moderating the excesses of the dominant cultural ethos and emphasizing its useful features, institutional reform can be stimulated, and significant reductions in crime can be realized.

We have characterized the American Dream as the commitment to the goal of monetary success, to be pursued by all members of society, under conditions of open, individual competition. The most important and valuable theme running through this cultural ethos is that of a universal entitlement to strive for a better life, which can be attained as a consequence of one's own achievements. In other words, the American Dream empowers everyone to dream about a brighter future and participate in the creation of that future. This vision of possibilities, of hope, is liberating, and it serves the interests of both individuals and the larger society by inspiring people to develop their talents and abilities.

The criminogenic tendencies of the American Dream derive from its *exaggerated* emphasis on monetary success and its resistance to limits on the means for the pursuit of success. Any significant lessening of the criminogenic consequences of the dominant culture thus requires the taming of its strong materialistic pressures and the creation of a greater receptivity to socially imposed restraints. To dampen the materialistic pressures, goals other than the accumulation of wealth will have to be elevated to a position of prominence in the cultural hierarchy. This implies greater recognition of and appreciation for the institutional realms that are currently subservient to the economy. More specifically, social roles such as parenting, "spousing," teaching, learning, and serving the community will have to become, as ends in themselves, meaningful alternatives to material acquisition. Furthermore, enhancing the respect for these noneconomic roles implies that money will no longer serve as the principal gauge of social achievement and personal worth. Money will not be, in the words of Marian Wright Edelman, the preeminent "measure of our success."[47]

The other, complementary task of cultural regeneration will involve fostering a cultural receptivity to restraints. The dominant cultural ethos glorifies the individual pursuit of material well-being. People are encouraged to maximize personal utility, to be guided by self-interest, and to regard others as potential competitors in the race for economic rewards. However, many of the institutional reforms to which we point entail the subordination of individual interests to larger collectivities, such as the family and the community. In short, it seems unlikely that social change conducive to lower levels of crime will occur in the absence of a cultural reorientation that encompasses an enhanced emphasis on the importance of mutual support and collective obligations and a decreased emphasis on individual rights, interests, and privileges.[48]

An Intellectual Foundation for Change

An important intellectual component accompanies the task of balancing social obligations with individual interests. The extreme individualism of American culture impedes a full understanding of the interdependencies between the individual and society. Human beings are inherently social beings. As a consequence, their individual development and maturation presuppose social relationships that are necessarily constraining. To borrow from Marx once again: "Only in association with others has each individual the means of cultivating his [or her] talents in all directions."[49]

The idea that individual growth requires social motivation, support, and regulation forms part of the distinctive corpus of classical sociological thought. It figures significantly not only in Marx's analysis of capitalist society but also in George Herbert Mead's theory of the social formation of the self and in Émile Durkheim's conception of the collective conscience.[50] It is one of the few ideas in the history of sociological thought that is not readily identified as belonging to one or another intellectual or ideological camp. It links the micro- and the macrolevels of analysis and informs conflict theories of social change as well as consensus theories of social order. As a defining element in the common heritage of the discipline, it prepares the conceptual ground for a sociological reappraisal of the American Dream.

This reappraisal suggests that different parts of the American Dream work at cross purposes. Its universalism and achievement orientation inspire ambition and in so doing stimulate the motivational dynamic necessary for the realization of human potential. However, its exaggerated materialism and extreme individualism narrow the range of human capacities that receive cultural respect and social support and discourage people from assuming obligations that in principle could be liberating. By clarifying this internal contradiction, a sociological understanding of the American Dream can help lay the intellectual groundwork for the cultural and institutional changes necessary for reducing crime in our society.

Toward a Mature Society

In closing, we return to James Truslow Adams for a final observation on the legacy and the future of the American Dream. Adams traces the possibilities of the Dream to the American Revolution. The cultural significance of the revolt lay in "the breaking down of all spiritual barriers to the complete development of whatever might prove to be fertile, true, and lasting in the American dream."[51] However, Adams laments the fact that this developmental potential was inhibited by the "debilitating doctrine" that, two centuries after its birth, the United States is still a "young" nation. He asks:

> Is it not time to proclaim that we are not children but men [and women] who must put away childish things; that we have overlooked that fact too long; that we·have busied ourselves overmuch with fixing up the new place we moved into 300 years ago, with making money in the new neighborhood; and that we should begin to live a sane, maturely civilized life?[52]

The promise of a mature America is the cultural encouragement for all persons to develop their full range of talents and capacities on the basis of mutual support and collective obligations. Adams' American Dream, and ours, must be reinvented so that its destructive consequences can be curbed, and so that its fertile, true, and lasting promise of human development can be fulfilled.

NOTES

1. Edelman (1992, p. 89).

2. "In Dreams Begin Responsibilities" is the title of Delmore Schwartz's short story originally published in *Partisan Review* in 1937. It is reprinted in Schwartz ([1937] 1978, pp. 1–9).

3. Adams ([1929] 1969, p. 143).

4. Adams ([1929] 1969, p. 122).

5. Adams ([1929] 1969, p. 123).

6. Adams ([1929] 1969, pp. 101, 116).

7. Adams ([1929] 1969, p. 142).

8. Adams ([1929] 1969, p. 143).

9. Blumstein (1993, p. 10). The NCRP data on prison admissions are reported in Bureau of Justice Statistics (1992b, p. 8).

10. Bureau of Justice Statistics (1995b, p. 8, Tables 10–11).

11. See Bureau of Justice Statistics (1995b, p. 7, Tables 8–9) for prison capacity data. The American Correctional Association's

capacity guidelines are reported in Schlesinger (1987, p. 1).

12. Bureau of Justice Statistics (1995a).

13. The percentage growth in correctional populations between 1980 and 1993 is reported in Bureau of Justice Statistics (1995a). The projections for the next century are based on growth rates in correctional populations during the mid-1980s. See Rosenfeld and Kempf (1991, pp. 488–489).

14. Blumstein (1993, p. 5). For a penetrating and disturbing discussion of the disparate impact of the drug war on African Americans, see Tonry (1995).

15. See Steinberg (1981, pp. 194–200) for a discussion of the role of the black codes in the "reconstruction of black servitude" after the Civil War.

16. See Blumstein (1995), Federal Bureau of Investigation (1992, pp. 279–289), and Tonry (1995).

17. See Walker (1989, pp. 153–159) for a review of arguments surrounding plea bargaining as an adaptation to large caseloads and for a discussion of realistic reforms of this widespread practice.

18. Feeley and Simon (1992).

19. For research on the relationship between sex ratios and family relations, see Messner and Sampson (1991) and South and Trent (1988). See also Sampson (1987) for evidence concerning the effects of family disruption on rates of black violence.

20. Quoted in Blumstein (1993, p. 11).

21. Cloward and Ohlin (1960).

22. See Liska (1987, p. 52) for a description of the Mobilization for Youth program and a discussion of research assessing its effectiveness.

23. Sidel (1986, p. 110).

24. See especially Wilson (1975, Chapter 1).

25. *Routine activities theory*, which links crime to variations in the behavior of victims rather than to the motivations of offenders, was introduced as a distinctive approach in criminology by Cohen and Felson (1979).

26. This point is elaborated in Rosenfeld (1989, pp. 459–462).

27. See Wilson (1987, especially Chapter 2).

28. Wilson (1975, p. 235).

29. Gilsinan (1990, pp. 5–6). For a historical perspective on the limits of the criminal justice system as a means of crime control, see Friedman (1993).

30. Berger (1963, p. 121).

31. Mansnerus (1993). Levitan, Belous, and Gallo (1988) provide an excellent overview of the relationship between the family and other institutions, and numerous proposals for strengthening family functioning.

32. Interview with Randall Curran reported in Mansnerus (1993, p. 14).

33. The data on birth and marriage rates are from U.S. Bureau of the Census (1991, p. 44, Table 52; p. 63, Table 84; 1994, p. 56, Table 60).

34. Murray (1994). The quotations are from pp. 9, 14, and 15.

35. For an extended discussion and critique of proposals to reform the public schools through the introduction of market mechanisms, see Henig (1994). Henig argues that advocates of market reform tend to ignore the collective purposes of education, and their market-based proposals often threaten to "erode the public forums in which decisions with societal consequences can democratically be resolved" (p. 200).

36. U.S. Bureau of the Census (1994, p. 157, Table 232).

37. The approach to correctional policy introduced in this section is discussed more fully in Rosenfeld and Kempf (1991).

38. On the conflicting goals of correctional policy, see Thomas (1987).

39. See Morris and Tonry (1990) for a discussion of the purposes and a hopeful appraisal of the prospects of intermediate sanctions. Byrne, Lurigio, and Petersilia (1992) assess a broad range of existing programs. The potential costs of intensified community supervision of offenders are discussed in Rosenfeld and Kempf (1991).

40. Rosenfeld and Kempf (1991, p. 492).

41. Klein (1992).

42. For a description of AmeriCorps as a crime prevention program, see President's Crime Prevention Council (1995).

43. See the "Critique of the Gotha Programme" in Marx and Engels (1968, pp. 315–335; quoted material is from p. 325).

44. Esping-Andersen (1990) reports decommodification scores in his incisive analysis of different welfare state regimes, *The Three Worlds of Welfare Capitalism*. Following conventional practice for dealing with highly skewed dependent variables in linear modeling, the homicide rates in Figure 5–1 are expressed in terms of natural logarithms. We also find an inverse relationship between decommodification and homicide rates in a multivariate analysis based on a larger sample of nations ($N = 45$). This analysis includes statistical controls for a wide range of demographic and socioeconomic characteristics of nations. See Messner and Rosenfeld (1994).

45. For thoughtful discussions of potential dangers for the balance among social institutions of the expansion of the welfare state, see Habermas (1989) and Wolfe (1989).

46. See Hochschild (1995, pp. 258–260) for a similar appraisal.

47. *The Measure of Our Success* is the title of Edelman's (1992) book from which her quotation at the beginning of this chapter is taken.

48. See Braithwaite (1989, pp. 168–174).

49. Quoted in Bottomore and Rubel (1964, p. 247). For a recent reaffirmation of this basic sociological premise, see Bellah, Madsen, Sullivan, Swidler, and Tipton (1991, p. 6).

50. Berger and Luckmann (1966) provide an excellent treatment of the "dialectic" between the individual and society.

51. Quoted in Nevins (1968, p. 70).

52. Adams ([1929] 1969, p. 256).

References

Adams, James Truslow. 1931. *The Epic of America*. Boston: Little, Brown.

———. [1929] 1969. *Our Business Civilization: Some Aspects of American Culture*. New York: AMS Press.

Adler, Freda. 1983. *Nations Not Obsessed with Crime*. Littleton, CO: Rothman.

Adler, Freda, and William S. Laufer. 1995. *The Legacy of Anomie Theory*. New Brunswick, NJ: Transaction.

Agnew, Robert. 1992. "Foundation for a General Strain Theory of Crime and Delinquency." *Criminology* 30:47–87.

Akers, Ronald L., Marvin D. Krohn, Lonn Lanza-Kaduce, and Marcia Radosevich. 1979. "Social Learning and Deviant Behavior." *American Sociological Review* 44:636–655.

Albany Times-Union. 1995. "Gingrich Promotes His Reading Program." March 2, p. A6.

Alter, Jonathan. 1992. "The Body Count at Home." *Newsweek*, December 28, p. 55.

———. 1993. "There's a War On at Home." *Newsweek*, September 27, p. 42.

Archer, Dane, and Rosemary Gartner. 1984. *Violence and Crime in Cross-National Perspective*. New Haven, CT: Yale University Press.

Babbie, Earl. 1992. *The Practice of Social Research*. 6th ed. Belmont, CA: Wadsworth.

Bailey, Kenneth D. 1987. *Methods of Social Research*. 3d ed. New York: Free Press.

Bassis, Michael S., Richard J. Gelles, and Ann Levine. 1991. *Sociology: An Introduction*. 4th ed. New York: McGraw-Hill.

Bayley, David H. 1991. *Forces of Order: Policing Modern Japan*. Berkeley: University of California Press.

Beck, Melinda. 1993. "Mary Poppins Speaks Out." *Newsweek*, February 22, pp. 66–68.

Bellah, Robert N., Richard Madsen, William M. Sullivan, Ann Swidler, and Steven M. Tipton. 1985. *Habits of the Heart: Individualism and Commitment in American Life*. Berkeley: University of California Press.

————. 1991. *The Good Society.* New York: Knopf.

Berger, Peter L. 1963. *Invitation to Sociology: A Humanistic Perspective.* Garden City, NY: Anchor.

Berger, Peter L., and Thomas Luckmann. 1966. *The Social Construction of Reality: A Treatise in the Sociology of Knowledge.* Garden City, NY: Anchor.

Berke, Richard L. 1993. "Check of Kimba Wood's Background Awaited." *New York Times,* February 5, pp. A1, A12.

Bernard, Thomas J. 1984. "Control Criticisms of Strain Theories: An Assessment of Theoretical and Empirical Adequacy." *Journal of Research in Crime and Delinquency* 21: 353–372.

————. 1995. "Merton Versus Hirschi: Who Is Faithful to Durkheim's Heritage?" Pages 81–90 in *The Legacy of Anomie Theory,* ed. Freda Adler and William S. Laufer. New Brunswick, NJ: Transaction.

Beutel, Ann M., and Margaret Mooney Marini. 1995. "Gender and Values." *American Sociological Review* 60: 436–448.

Biderman, Albert D., and James P. Lynch. 1991. *Understanding Crime Incidence Statistics: Why the UCR Diverges from the NCS.* New York: Springer.

Black, Donald. 1984. "Crime as Social Control." Pages 1–27 in *Toward a General Theory of Social Control,* vol. 2, ed. by Donald Black. New York: Academic Press.

Blau, Peter M., and Judith R. Blau. 1982. "The Cost of Inequality: Metropolitan Structure and Violent Crime." *American Sociological Review* 47: 114–129.

Blumstein, Alfred. 1993. "Making Rationality Relevant—The American Society of Criminology 1992 Presidential Address." *Criminology* 31: 1–16.

————. 1995. "Youth Violence, Guns and the Illicit-Drug Industry." *Journal of Criminal Law and Criminology* 86: 10–36.

Bohlen, Celestine. 1996. "Where Everyday Is Mother's Day." *New York Times,* May 12, section 4, pp. 1–5.

Bottomore, T. B., and Maximilien Rubel. 1964. *Karl Marx: Selected Writings in Sociology and Social Philosophy.* New York: McGraw-Hill.

Bradsher, Keith. 1990. "Judge with a Reputation for Innovative Rulings." *New York Times,* November 22, p. D5.

————. 1995. "Low Ranking for Poor American Children." *New York Times,* August 14, p. A7.

Braithwaite, John. 1989. *Crime, Shame and Reintegration.* New York: Cambridge University Press.

Bryan, Bill. 1992. "Neighborhood Crime Takes Deadly Toll: Elderly Man Dies After Robbery." *St. Louis Post-Dispatch,* August 25, p. 3A.

————. 1996. "Shooting Victim Was Help to Many." *St. Louis Post-Dispatch,* February 27, pp. 1A, 5A.

Bryan, Bill, and Joan Little. 1993. "Student, 17, Fatally Shot at Sumner." *St. Louis Post-Dispatch,* March 26, pp. 1A, 10A.

Bureau of Justice Statistics. 1992a. *Criminal Victimization in the United States, 1991.* Washington, D.C.: U.S. Department of Justice.

————. 1992b. *Prisoners in 1991.* Washington, D.C.: U.S. Department of Justice.

————. 1995a. *Correctional Populations in the United States.* Washington, D.C.: U.S. Department of Justice.

————. 1995b. *Prisoners in 1994.* Washington, D.C.: U.S. Department of Justice.

Burgess, Robert L., and Ronald L. Akers. 1966. "A Differential Association-Reinforcement Theory of Criminal Behavior." *Social Problems* 14: 128–147.

Bursik, Robert J., Jr. 1988. "Social Disorganization and Theories of Crime and Delinquency: Problems and Prospects." *Criminology* 26: 519–551.

Bursik, Robert J., and Harold Grasmick. 1993. *Neighborhoods and Crime: The Dimensions of Effective Community Control.* New York: Lexington Books.

Burton, Velmer S., Jr., and Francis T. Cullen. 1992. "The Empirical Status of Strain Theory." *Journal of Crime and Justice* 15: 1–30.

Byrne, James M., Arthur J. Lurigio, and Joan Petersilia, eds. 1992. *Smart Sentencing: The Emergence of Intermediate Sanctions.* Newbury Park, CA: Sage.

Calavita, Kitty, and Henry N. Pontell. 1991. " 'Other's People's Money' Revisited: Collective Embezzlement in the Savings and Loan and Insurance Industries." *Social Problems* 38: 94–112.

Chamlin, Mitchell B., and John K. Cochran. 1995. "Assessing Messner and Rosenfeld's Institutional Anomie Theory: A Partial Test." *Criminology* 33: 411–429.

———. 1996. "Reply to Jensen." *Criminology* 34: 133–134.

Centers for Disease Control. 1991. "Forum on Youth Violence in Minority Communities: Setting the Agenda for Prevention. Summary of the Proceedings." *Public Health Reports* 106: 225–279.

Chapman, Stephen. 1992. "LA Jurors Blinded by Fear of Crime." *St. Louis Post-Dispatch*, May 4, p. 3B.

Cherlin, Andrew J. 1992. *Marriage, Divorce, Remarriage.* Revised and enlarged ed. Cambridge, MA: Harvard University Press.

Chicago Tribune. 1991. "Englewood Longs for the Safe Old Days." December 29, section 2, pp. 1–3.

Clinard, Marshall B., ed. 1964. *Anomie and Deviant Behavior: A Discussion and Critique.* New York: Free Press.

Clinard, Marshall B., and Peter C. Yeager. 1980. *Corporate Crime.* New York: Free Press.

Clines, Francis X. 1993. "An Unfettered Milken Has Lessons to Teach." *New York Times*, October 16, pp. 1, 9.

Cloward, Richard, and Lloyd E. Ohlin. 1960. *Delinquency and Opportunity: A Theory of Delinquent Gangs.* New York: Free Press.

Cohen, Albert K. 1955. *Delinquent Boys: The Culture of the Gang.* Glencoe, IL: Free Press.

———. 1985. "The Assumption That Crime Is a Product of Environments: Sociological Approaches." pp. 223–243 in *Theoretical Methods in Criminology*, ed. Robert F. Meier. Beverly Hills: Sage.

Cohen, Deborah Vidaver. 1995. "Ethics and Crime in Business Firms: Organizational Culture and the Impact of Anomie." pp. 183–206 in *The Legacy of Anomie Theory*, ed. Freda Adler and William S. Laufer. New Brunswick NJ: Transaction.

Cohen, Lawrence E., and Marcus Felson. 1979. "Social Change and Crime Rate Trends: A Routine Activities Approach." *American Sociological Review* 44: 588–608.

Cole, Stephen. 1975. "The Growth of Scientific Knowledge: Theories of Deviance as a Case Study." pp. 175–220 in *The Idea of Social Structure: Papers in Honor of Robert K. Merton*, ed. Lewis A. Coser. New York: Harcourt Brace Jovanovich.

Coleman, James William. 1994. *The Criminal Elite: The Sociology of White Collar Crime.* 3d ed. New York: St. Martin's Press.

Coleman, Richard P., and Lee Rainwater. 1978. *Social Standing in America: New Dimensions of Class.* New York: Basic Books.

Colvin, Mark, and John Pauly. 1983. "A Critique of Criminology: Toward an Integrated Structural-Marxist Theory of Delinquency Production." *American Journal of Sociology* 89: 513–551.

Cullen, Francis T. 1983. *Rethinking Crime and Deviance Theory: The Emergence of a Structuring Tradition.* Totowa, NJ: Rowman & Allanheld.

———. 1988. "Were Cloward and Ohlin Strain Theorists? Delinquency and Opportunity Revisited." *Journal of Research in Crime and Delinquency* 25: 214–241.

Currie, Elliott. 1991. "Crime in the Market Society: From Bad to Worse in the Nineties." *Dissent* (Spring): 254–259.

Curtis, Lynn A. 1975. *Violence, Race, and Culture.* Lexington, MA: Heath.

Derber, Charles. 1992. *Money, Murder and the American Dream: Wilding from Main Street to Wall Street.* Boston: Faber & Faber.

———. 1996. *The Wilding of America: How Greed and Violence Are Eroding Our Nation's Character.* New York: St. Martin's.

Dershowitz, Alan M. 1992. "The Arrogant Media." *Albany Times Union,* September 7, p. A6.

Dobrin, Adam, Brian Wiersema, Colin Loftin, and David McDowall. 1996. *Statistical Handbook on Violence in America.* Phoenix: Oryx.

Downes, David, and Paul Rock. 1982. *Understanding Deviance: A Guide to the Sociology of Crime and Rule Breaking.* Oxford: Clarendon.

Durkheim, Émile. [1893] 1964a. *The Division of Labor in Society.* New York: Free Press.

———. [1895] 1964b. *The Rules of Sociological Method.* New York: Free Press.

———. [1897] 1966. *Suicide: A Study in Sociology.* New York: Free Press.

Edelman, Marian Wright. 1992. *The Measure of Our Success: A Letter to My Children and Yours.* Boston: Beacon.

Edsall, Thomas Byrne. 1992. "Willie Horton's Message." *New York Review,* February 13, pp. 7–11.

Eichenwald, Kurt. 1990. "Milken Gets Ten Years for Wall St. Crimes." *New York Times,* November 22, pp. A1, D5.

Elkins, Stanley M. 1968. *Slavery: A Problem in American Institutional and Intellectual Life.* 2d ed. Chicago: University of Chicago Press.

Elliott, Delbert, David Huizinga, and Suzanne Ageton. 1985. *Explaining Delinquency and Drug Use.* Beverly Hills: Sage.

Erikson, Kai T. 1966. *Wayward Puritans: A Study in the Sociology of Deviance.* New York: Wiley.

Ermann, M. David, and Richard J. Lundman. 1982. *Corporate Deviance.* New York: Holt, Rinehart & Winston.

———. 1987. *Corporate and Governmental Deviance.* New York: Oxford.

Esping-Andersen, Gosta. 1990. *The Three Worlds of Welfare Capitalism.* Princeton, NJ: Princeton University Press.

Farnworth, Margaret, and Michael J. Lieber. 1989. "Strain Theory Revisited: Economic Goals, Educational Means, and Delinquency." *American Sociological Review* 54: 263–274.

Farrell, Ronald A., and Victoria L. Swigert. 1985. "The Corporation in Criminology: New Directions for Research." *Journal of Research in Crime and Delinquency* 22: 83–94.

Federal Bureau of Investigation. 1993a. *Age-Specific Arrest Rates and Race-Specific Arrest Rates for Selected Offenses 1965–1992.* Washington, D.C.: U.S. Department of Justice.

———. 1991. *Crime in the United States.* Washington, D.C.: U.S. Government Printing Office.

———. 1993b. *Crime in the United States.* Washington, D.C.: U.S. Government Printing Office.

Feeley, Malcolm M., and Jonathan Simon. 1992. "The New Penology: Notes on the Emerging Strategy of Corrections and Its Implications." *Criminology* 30: 449–474.

Fingerhut, Lois A., and Joel C. Kleinman. 1990. "International and Interstate Comparisons of Homicide Among Young Males." *Journal of the American Medical Association* 263: 3292–3295.

Fishbein, Diana H. 1990. "Biological Perspectives in Criminology." *Criminology* 28 (February): 27–72.

Folbre, Nancy. 1992. "Business to the Rescue?" *The Nation,* September 21, pp. 281–282.

Friedman, Lawrence M. 1993. *Crime and Punishment in American History.* New York: Basic Books.

Friedman, Thomas L. 1996. "Japan Inc. Revisited." *New York Times,* February 25, p. E15.

Gastil, Raymond D. 1971. "Homicide and a Regional Culture of Violence." *American Sociological Review* 36: 412–427.

Gibbons, Don C. 1992. *Society, Crime, and Criminal Behavior.* 6th ed. Upper Saddle River, NJ: Prentice Hall.

Gilsinan, James F. 1990. *Criminology and Public Policy.* Upper Saddle River, NJ: Prentice Hall.

Gottfredson, Michael R., and Travis Hirschi. 1990. *A General Theory of Crime.* Stanford, CA: Stanford University Press.

Gouldner, Alvin W. 1970. *The Coming Crisis of Western Sociology.* New York: Basic Books.

Gove, Walter R., Michael Hughes, and Michael Geerken. 1985. "Are Uniform Crime Reports a Valid Indicator of the Index Crimes? An Affirmative Answer with Minor Qualifications." *Criminology* 23:451–501.

Gurr, Ted Robert. 1989. "Historical Trends in Violent Crime: Europe and the United States." pp. 21–54 in *Violence in America*, vol. 1: *The History of Crime*, ed. Ted R. Gurr. Newbury Park, CA: Sage.

Gutman, Herbert G. 1976. *The Black Family in Slavery and Freedom, 1750–1925.* New York: Vintage.

Habermas, Jurgen. 1989. "The Crisis of the Welfare State and the Exhaustion of Utopian Energies." pp. 284–299 in *Jurgen Habermas on Society and Politics: A Reader*, ed. Steven Seidman. Boston: Beacon.

Hacker, Andrew. 1992. *Two Nations: Black and White, Separate, Hostile, Unequal.* New York: Scribner's.

Hackney, Sheldon. 1969. "Southern Violence." pp. 505–528 in *History of Violence in America: Report of the Task Force on Historical and Comparative Perspectives to the National Commission on the Causes and Prevention of Violence*, ed. Hugh D. Graham and Ted R. Gurr. New York: Bantam.

Hagan, Frank. 1992. "From HUD to Iran-Contra: Crime During the Reagan Administration." Paper presented at the Forty-fourth Annual Meeting of the American Society of Criminology, New Orleans, LA, November 4–7.

Hagan, John, John Simpson, and A. R. Gillis. 1987. "Class in the Household: A Power-Control Theory of Gender and Delinquency." *American Journal of Sociology* 92: 788–816.

Hancock, Lyn Nell (with Claudia Kalb). 1995. "Returned for Credit." *Newsweek*, May 22, p. 44.

Harris, Marvin. 1981. *America Now: The Anthropology of a Changing Culture.* New York: Simon & Schuster.

Harrison, Bennett, and Barry Bluestone. 1988. *The Great U-Turn: Corporate Restructuring and the Polarizing of America.* New York: Basic Books.

Hawley, F. Frederick, and Steven F. Messner. 1989. "The Southern Violence Construct: A Review of Arguments, Evidence, and the Normative Context." *Justice Quarterly* 6: 481–511.

Hearn, Charles R. 1977. *The American Dream in the Great Depression.* Westport, CT: Greenwood.

Heilbroner, Robert. 1991. "A Pivotal Question Unanswered." *The World & I: A Chronicle of our Changing Era* (November): 538–540.

Henig, Jeffrey R. 1994. *Rethinking School Choice: Limits of the Market Metaphor.* Princeton, NJ: Princeton University Press.

Hernon, Peter. 1992. "Amid Reality of Nightly Gunfights, Residents Stay Committed to Area." *St. Louis Post-Dispatch*, October 4, pp. 1A, 9A.

Hirschi, Travis. 1969. *Causes of Delinquency.* Berkeley: University of California Press.

———. 1979. "Separate and Unequal Is Better." *Journal of Research in Crime and Delinquency* 16: 34–38.

———. 1989. "Exploring Alternatives to Integrated Theory." pp. 37–49 in *Theoretical Integration in the Study of Deviance and Crime: Problems and Prospects*, ed. Steven F. Messner, Marvin D. Krohn, and Allen E. Liska. Albany: State University of New York Press.

Hobbes, Thomas. [1651] 1958. *Leviathan.* Indianapolis, IN: Bobbs-Merrill.

Hochschild, Arlie. 1989. *The Second Shift.* New York: Avon Books.

Hochschild, Jennifer. 1995. *Facing Up to the American Dream: Race, Class, and the Soul of the Nation.* Princeton, NJ: Princeton University Press.

Hodgins, Sheilagh. 1992. "Mental Disorder, Intellectual Deficiency, and Crime." *Archives of General Psychiatry* 49: 476–483.

Interpol. 1991–92. *International Crime Statistics.* Saint Cloud, France: International Criminal Police Organization.

Jensen, Gary F. 1996. "Comment on Chamlin and Cochran." *Criminology* 34:129–131.

Johannesburg Star. 1996. "SA Set to Keep Dubious Title of 'Murder Capital of the World.'" January 10.

Johnson, Allan G. 1991. *The Forest for the Trees: An Introduction to Sociological Thinking.* San Diego, CA: Harcourt Brace Jovanovich.

Kalish, Carol B. 1988. *International Crime Rates.* Washington, D.C.: U.S. Department of Justice.

Kappeler, Victor E., Mark Blumberg, and Gary W. Potter. 1993. *The Mythology of Crime and Criminal Justice.* Prospect Heights, IL: Waveland.

Kates, Don B., Jr. 1989. "Firearms and Violence: Old Premises and Current Evidence." pp. 197–215 in *Violence in America*, vol. 1: *The History of Crime*, ed. Ted R. Gurr. Newbury Park, CA: Sage.

Keillor, Garrison. 1992. "Enjoy." *New York Times*, July 13, p. A15.

Kleck, Gary. 1991. *Point Blank: Guns and Violence in America.* Hawthorne, NY: Aldine.

Klein, Joe. 1992. "Copping a Domestic Agenda." *Newsweek*, December 7, p. 29.

Kornhauser, Ruth R. 1978. *Social Sources of Delinquency: An Appraisal of Analytic Models.* Chicago: University of Chicago Press.

Kozol, Jonathan. 1991. *Savage Inequalities: Children in America's Schools.* New York: Crown.

———. 1992. "Whittle and the Privateers." *The Nation*, September 21, pp. 272–278.

Kroeber, A. L., and Talcott Parsons. 1958. "The Concepts of Culture and of Social System." *American Sociological Review* 23: 582–583.

LaFree, Gary D., and Edward L. Kick. 1986. "Cross-National Effects of Developmental, Distributional, and Demographic Variables on Crime: A Review and Analysis." *International Annals of Criminology* 24: 213–235.

Lane, Ann J., ed. 1971. *The Debate over Slavery: Stanley Elkins and His Critics.* Urbana: University of Illinois Press.

Lasch, Christopher. 1977. *Haven in a Heartless World: The Family Besieged.* New York: Basic Books.

Lemert, Edwin M. 1964. "Social Structure, Social Control, and Deviation." pp. 57–97 in *Anomie and Deviant Behavior*, ed. Marshall B. Clinard. New York: Free Press.

Levitan, Sar A., Richard S. Belous, and Frank Gallo. 1988. *What's Happening to the American Family?* Baltimore: Johns Hopkins University Press.

Levy, Frank. 1988. *Dollars and Dreams.* New York: Norton.

Lewis, Michael. 1990. "Milken's Morals, and Ours." *New York Times*, November 21, p. A23.

Lewis, Oscar. 1966. "The Culture of Poverty." *Scientific American* 215: 19–25.

Lilly, J. Robert, Francis T. Cullen, and Richard A. Ball. 1989. *Criminological Theory: Context and Consequences.* Newbury Park, CA: Sage.

Liska, Allen E. 1987. *Perspectives on Deviance.* 2d ed. Upper Saddle River, NJ: Prentice Hall.

Little, Joan. 1992. "Wisconsin Man Is Held in Bilking of Elderly." *St. Louis Post-Dispatch*, August 25, p. 5A.

———. 1994. "Pupils Told to 'Run for Your Lives.'" *St. Louis Post-Dispatch*, February 22, pp. 1A, 8A.

Long, Elizabeth. 1985. *The American Dream and the Popular Novel.* Boston: Routledge & Kegan Paul.

Lynch, James. 1995. "Crime in International Perspective." Pages 11–38 in *Crime*, ed. James Q. Wilson and Joan Petersilia. San Francisco: ICS.

MacKenzie, Doris Layton, Phyllis Jo Baunach, and Roy R. Roberg, eds. 1990. *Measuring Crime: Large-Scale, Long-Range Efforts*. Albany: State University of New York Press.

MacLeod, Jay. 1987. *Ain't No Makin' It: Leveled Aspirations in a Low-Income Neighborhood*. Boulder, CO: Westview.

Maguire, Kathleen, and Ann L. Pastore. 1995. *Sourcebook of Criminal Justice Statistics, 1994*. Washington, D.C.: U.S. Government Printing Office.

Mansnerus, Laura. 1993. "Kids of the 90's: A Bolder Breed." *New York Times*, April 4, Section 4A, pp. 14–15.

Marriott, Michel. 1995. "Living in 'Lockdown.' " *Newsweek*, January 23, pp. 56–57.

Martinez-Schnell, Beverly, and Richard J. Waxweiler. 1989. "Increases in Premature Mortality Due to Homicide— United States, 1968–1985." *Violence and Victims* 4:287–293.

Marx, Karl, and Frederick Engels. 1968. *Selected Works*. New York: International Publishers.

Massey, Douglas S., and Nancy Denton. 1993. *American Apartheid: Segregation and the Making of the Underclass*. Cambridge, MA: Harvard University Press.

Mauer, Marc. 1991. *Americans Behind Bars: A Comparison of International Rates of Incarceration*. Washington, D.C.: The Sentencing Project.

Mauer, Marc, and Tracy Huling. 1995. *Young Black Americans in the Criminal Justice System: Five Years Later*. Washington, D.C.: The Sentencing Project.

Mayhew, Pat. 1993. "American Crime Rates Not Highest." *Overcrowded Times* 4: 1, 8–11.

Menard, Scott. 1995. "A Developmental Test of Mertonian Anomie Theory." *Journal of Research in Crime and Delinquency* 32: 136–174.

Merton, Robert K. 1938. "Social Structure and Anomie." *American Sociological Review* 3: 672–682.

————. 1959. "Social Conformity, Deviation, and Opportunity Structures: A Comment on the Contributions of Dubin and Cloward." *American Sociological Review* 24: 177–189.

————. 1964. "Anomie, Anomia, and Social Interaction." pp. 213–242 in *Anomie and Deviant Behavior*, ed. Marshall Clinard. New York: Free Press.

————. 1968. *Social Theory and Social Structure*. New York: Free Press.

Messner, Steven F. 1988. "Merton's 'Social Structure and Anomie': The Road Not Taken." *Deviant Behavior* 9: 33–53.

Messner, Steven F., and Reid M. Golden. 1992. "Racial Inequality and Racially Disaggregated Crime Rates: An Assessment of Alternative Theoretical Explanations." *Criminology* 30: 421–445.

Messner, Steven F., and Richard Rosenfeld. 1994. "Political Restraint of the Market and Levels of Lethal Violence: A Cross-National Application of Institutional-Anomie Theory." Paper presented at the 46th Annual Meeting of the American Society of Criminology, Miami, FL, November 9–12.

————. 1996. "An Institutional-Anomie Theory of the Social Distribution of Crime." In *Contemporary Criminological Theory*, ed. Larry J. Siegel and Peter Cordella. Boston: Northeastern University Press (in press).

Messner, Steven F., and Robert J. Sampson. 1991. "The Sex Ratio, Family Disruption, and Rates of Violent Crime: The Paradox of Demographic Structure." *Social Forces* 69: 693–713.

Miller, Jerome. 1992. *Hobbling a Generation: Young African-American Males in D.C.'s Criminal Justice System*. Alexandria, VA: National Center on Institutions and Alternatives.

Miller, Ted R., Mark A. Cohen, and Brian Wiersema. 1996. *Victim Costs and Consequences: A New Look*. Washington, D.C.: U.S. Department of Justice.

Miller, Walter B. 1958. "Lower Class Culture as a Generating Milieu of Gang Delinquency." *Journal of Social Issues* 14: 5–19.

Mills, C. Wright. 1943. "The Professional Ideology of Social Pathologists." *American Journal of Sociology* 49: 165–180.

Morris, Norval, and Michael Tonry. 1990. *Between Prison and Probation: Intermediate Punishments in a Rational Sentencing System.* New York: Oxford University Press.

Mortenson, Tom. 1996. "Black Men in College or Behind Bars." *Overcrowded Times* 7: 2.

Murray, David W. 1994. "Poor Suffering Bastards." *Policy Review* (Spring): 9–15.

Mydans, Seth. 1993. "Korean Shop Owners Fearful of Outcome of Beating Trial." *New York Times,* April 10, pp. 1, 12.

Neuman, W. Lawrence, and Ronald J. Berger. 1988. "Competing Perspectives on Cross-National Crime: An Evaluation of Theory and Evidence." *Sociological Quarterly* 29: 281–313.

Nevins, Allan. 1968. *James Truslow Adams: Historian of the American Dream.* Urbana: University of Illinois Press.

Newsweek. 1992. "U.S. Troops: Black Like Me" December 21, p. 29.

New York Times. 1990a. "Stunning Justice in the Milken Case." November 22, p. A26.

———. 1990b. "Too Much Milken Moralizing." November 27, p. A22.

———. 1992. "A Downgraded Detroit Cries Foul." November 3, pp. C1, C4.

———. 1994. "Clinton Urges Quick Passage for Crime Bill." June 6, p. A9.

———. 1995. "Retirees Help in Roundup of Suspects in Vast Phone Fraud." December 8, p. A16.

———. 1996. "Murder Rate Has Soared in South Africa." April 18, p. A7.

Nightingale, Carl Husemoller. 1993. *On the Edge: A History of Poor Black Children and Their American Dreams.* New York: Basic Books.

Nisbet, Robert. 1971. "The Study of Social Problems." pp. 1–25 in *Contemporary Social Problems,* 3d ed., ed. Robert K. Merton and Robert Nisbet. New York: Harcourt Brace Jovanovich.

O'Brien, Robert M. 1985. *Crime and Victimization Data.* Beverly Hills: Sage.

O'Connor, John J. 1993. "TV Likes to Explore Violence That May Inspire." *New York Times,* December 9, p. B3.

Orru, Marco. 1987. *Anomie: History and Meanings.* Boston: Allen & Unwin.

———. 1990. "Merton's Instrumental Theory of Anomie." pp. 231–240 in *Robert K. Merton: Consensus and Controversy,* ed. Jon Clark, Celia Modgil, and Sohan Modgil. London: Falmer.

Park, Robert E., Ernest W. Burgess, and Roderick D. McKenzie. [1925] 1967. *The City.* Chicago: University of Chicago Press.

Parsons, Talcott. 1951. *The Social System.* New York: Free Press.

———. 1964. *Essays in Sociological Theory.* Rev. ed. New York: Free Press.

Passas, Nikos. 1990. "Anomie and Corporate Deviance." *Contemporary Crises* 14: 157–178.

Pfohl, Stephen J. 1985. *Images of Deviance and Social Control: A Sociological History.* New York: McGraw-Hill.

Polanyi, Karl. [1944] 1957. *The Great Transformation: The Political and Economic Origins of Our Time.* Boston: Beacon.

President's Crime Prevention Council. 1995. *Preventing Crime and Promoting Responsibility.* Washington, D.C.: U.S. Government Printing Office.

Rainwater, Lee. 1974. *What Money Buys: Inequality and the Social Meanings of Income.* New York: Basic Books.

Reiss, Albert J., Jr., and Jeffrey A. Roth, eds. 1993. *Understanding and Preventing Violence.* Washington, D.C.: National Academy Press.

Reichel, Philip L. 1994. *Comparative Criminal Justice Systems.* Upper Saddle River, NJ: Prentice Hall.

Reuter, Peter. 1984. "Social Control in Illegal Markets." pp. 29–58 in *Toward a General Theory of Social Control,* vol. 2, ed. Donald Black. New York: Academic Press.

Richardson, Lynda. 1992. "Somalia? In the South Bronx, They Ask, Why Not Aid Us?" *New York Times,* December 14, p. A8.

Robinson, Michael A. 1990. *Overdrawn: The Bailout of American Savings.* New York: Penguin.

Ropers, Richard H. 1991. *Persistent Poverty: The American Dream Turned Nightmare.* New York: Plenum.

Rosenberg, Mark L., and James A. Mercy. 1986. "Homicide: Epidemiologic Analysis at the National Level." *Bulletin of the New York Academy of Medicine* 62: 376–399.

Rosenfeld, Richard. 1989. "Robert Merton's Contributions to the Sociology of Deviance." *Sociological Inquiry* 59: 453–466.

———. 1991. "Anatomy of the Drug-Related Homicide." pp. 3.1–3.25 in *St. Louis Homicide Project: Local Responses to a National Problem,* ed. Scott H. Decker, Carol Kohfeld, Richard Rosenfeld, and John Sprague. St. Louis: University of Missouri–St. Louis.

Rosenfeld, Richard, and Scott Decker. 1993. "Where Public Health and Law Enforcement Meet: Monitoring and Preventing Youth Violence." *American Journal of Police* 12: 11–57.

Rosenfeld, Richard, and Kimberly F. Kempf. 1991. "The Scope and Purposes of Corrections: Exploring Alternative Responses to Crowding." *Crime and Delinquency* 37: 481–505.

Rosenfeld, Richard, and Steven F. Messner. 1995. "Consumption and Crime: An Institutional Inquiry." Paper presented at the Annual Meeting of the Academy of Criminal Justice Sciences, Boston, March 7–11.

———. 1996. "Markets, Morality, and an Institutional-Anomie Theory of Crime." In *The Future of Anomie Theory,* ed. Robert Agnew and Nikos Passas. Boston: Northeastern University Press (in press).

Rossi, Peter H., Emily Waite, Christine E. Bose, and Richard E. Berk. 1974. "The Seriousness of Crimes: Normative Structure and Individual Differences." *American Sociological Review* 39: 224–237.

Sampson, Robert J. 1987. "Urban Black Violence: The Effect of Male Joblessness and Family Disruption." *American Journal of Sociology* 93: 348–382.

Sampson, Robert J., and W. Byron Groves. 1989. "Community Structure and Crime: Testing Social-Disorganization Theory." *American Journal of Sociology* 94: 774–802.

Samuelson, Paul A., and William D. Nordhaus. 1989. *Macroeconomics: A Version of Economics.* 13th ed. New York: McGraw-Hill.

Samuelson, Robert J. 1992. "How Our American Dream Unraveled." *Newsweek,* March 2, pp. 32–39.

Sanger, David E. 1992. "As Gun Ban Erodes, Japanese Worry." *New York Times,* July 13, p. A3.

———. 1993. "After Gunman's Acquittal, Japan Struggles to Understand America." *New York Times,* May 25, pp. A1, A7.

———. 1994. "2 Students' Killings in California Confirm Fear of America in Japan." *New York Times,* March 29, pp. A1, A10.

Schlesinger, Steven R. 1987. "Prison Crowding in the United States: The Data." *Criminal Justice Research Bulletin* 3: 1–3.

Schur, Edwin M. 1969. *Our Criminal Society: The Social and Legal Sources of Crime in America.* Upper Saddle River, NJ: Prentice Hall.

Schwartz, Barry. 1994a. "On Morals and Markets." *Criminal Justice Ethics* 13: 61–69.

———. 1994b. *The Costs of Living: How Market Freedom Erodes the Best Things in Life.* New York: Norton.

Schwartz, Delmore. [1937] 1978. *In Dreams Begin Responsibilities and Other Stories.* New York: New Directions.

Schwarz, Benjamin. 1995/96. "Reflections on Inequality: 'The Promise of American Life.'" *World Policy Journal* 12: 33–39.

Sellin, Thorsten, and Marvin Wolfgang. 1964. *The Measurement of Delinquency.* New York: Wiley.

Shaw, Clifford R., and Henry D. McKay. 1969. *Juvenile Delinquency in Urban Areas*. Rev. ed. Chicago: University of Chicago Press.

Shelley, Louise I. 1981. *Crime and Modernization: The Impact of Industrialization and Urbanization on Crime*. Carbondale: Southern Illinois University Press.

Short, James F., Jr. 1985. "The Level of Explanation Problem in Criminology." pp. 51–72 in *Theoretical Methods in Criminology*, ed. Robert F. Meier. Beverly Hills: Sage.

Sidel, Ruth. 1986. *Women and Children Last: The Plight of Poor Women in Affluent America*. New York: Penguin Books.

Simon, David R. 1996. *Elite Deviance*. 5th ed. Boston: Allyn & Bacon.

Skogan, Wesley G. 1990. *Disorder and Decline: Crime and the Spiral of Decay in American Neighborhoods*. Berkeley: University of California Press.

Snyder, James, and Gerald Patterson. 1987. "Family Interaction and Delinquent Behavior." pp. 216–243 in *Handbook of Juvenile Delinquency*, ed. Herbert C. Quay. New York: Wiley.

Soll, Rick. 1993. "The Killing Fields." *Chicago* (March): 54–59, 97–99.

South, Scott J., and Katherine Trent. 1988. "Sex Ratios and Women's Roles: A Cross-National Analysis." *American Journal of Sociology* 93: 1096–1115.

St. Louis Post-Dispatch. 1992a. "Lithuania Is a Snap for U.S." August 7, p. D1.

———. 1992b. "More Young Families Are Poor, Study Finds" April 15, p. 11A.

Staples, Brent. 1993. "Confronting Slaughter in the Streets." *New York Times*, November 5, p. A12.

Staples, Robert. 1987. *The Urban Plantation: Racism and Colonialism in the Post Civil Rights Era*. Oakland, CA: Black Scholar Press.

Stark, Rodney. 1987. "Deviant Paces: A Theory of the Ecology of Crime." *Criminology* 25: 893–909.

Stark, Rodney, Lori Kent, and Daniel P. Doyle. 1982. "Religion and Delinquency: The Ecology of a 'Lost' Relationship." *Journal of Research in Crime and Delinquency* 19:4–24.

Steffensmeier, Darrell, and Emilie Allan. 1995. "Criminal Behavior: Gender and Age." pp. 83–113 in *Criminology*, ed. Joseph F. Sheley. Belmont, CA: Wadsworth.

Steinberg, Stephen. 1981. *The Ethnic Myth: Race, Ethnicity, and Class in America*. New York: Atheneum.

Stewart, James B. 1991. *Den of Thieves*. New York: Simon & Schuster.

Steyer, Robert. 1995. "OSHA Fines Clark in Fatal Blast." *St. Louis Post-Dispatch*, September 14, pp. 1C, 5C.

Stitt, B. Grant, and David J. Giacopassi. 1992. "Trends in the Connectivity of Theory and Research in Criminology." *The Criminologist* 17: 1, 3–6.

Sullivan, Ronald. 1992. "Milken's Sentence Reduced by Judge; 7 Months Are Left," *New York Times*, August 6, pp. A1, D17.

Surette, Ray. 1992. *Media, Crime, and Criminal Justice: Images and Realities*. Pacific Grove, CA: Brooks/Cole.

Sutherland, Edwin H. 1947. *Principles of Criminology*. Philadelphia: Lippincott.

———. 1949. *White Collar Crime*. New York: Holt, Rinehart & Winston.

Sykes, Gresham M., and Francis T. Cullen. 1992. *Criminology*. 2d ed. New York: Harcourt, Brace, Jovanovich.

Taylor, Ian, Paul Walton, and Jock Young. 1973. *The New Criminology: For a Social Theory of Deviance*. New York: Harper & Row.

Terry, Don. 1992. "Where Even a Grade School Is No Refuge from Gunfire." *New York Times*, October 17, p. A1, A6.

Tetzeli, Rick. 1992. "Most Dangerous and Endangered." *Fortune*, August 10, pp. 78–81.

Thomas, Charles W. 1987. *Corrections in America: Problems of the Past and the Present*. Newbury Park, CA: Sage.

Thompson, Linda, and Alexis J. Walker. 1991. "Gender in Families: Women and Men in Marriage, Work, and Parenthood." pp. 76–102 in *Contemporary Families: Looking Forward,*

Looking Back, ed. Alan Booth. Minneapolis: National Council on Family Relations.

Thomson, Susan C. 1992. "Job Oriented Courses Fuel Boom in Students at Private Colleges." *St. Louis Post-Dispatch*, December 8, p. 3A.

Tonry, Michael. 1995. *Malign Neglect: Race, Crime, and Punishment in America.* New York: Oxford.

Truell, Peter. 1995. "Milken, Barred as Financier, Puts His Stamp on Big Deals," *New York Times*, October 1, pp. 1, 20.

Turk, Austin T. 1969. *Criminality and Legal Order.* Chicago: Rand-McNally.

Turner, Jonathan H. 1978. *The Structure of Sociological Theory.* Rev. ed. Homewood, IL: Dorsey.

Turner, Jonathan H., and David Musick. 1985. *American Dilemmas: A Sociological Interpretation of Enduring Social Issues.* New York: Columbia University Press.

U.S. Bureau of the Census. 1991. *Statistical Abstract of the United States: 1991.* 111th ed. Washington, D.C.: U.S. Government Printing Office.

———. 1994. *Statistical Abstract of the United States: 1994.* 114th ed. Springfield, VA: National Technical Information Service.

———. 1995. *Statistical Abstract of the United States: 1995.* 115th ed. Springfield, VA: National Technical Information Service.

U.S. Congress House Committee on Government Operations. 1988. *Combatting Fraud, Abuse, and Misconduct in the Nation's Financial Institutions: Current Federal Efforts Are Inadequate*, Report Number 100-1088 and Errata. Washington, D.C.: U.S. Government Printing Office.

U.S. Public Health Service. 1990. *Healthy People 2000: National Health Promotion and Disease Prevention Objectives.* Washington, D.C.: U.S. Government Printing Office.

van den Haag, Ernest. 1978. "No Excuse for Crime." Pages 205–211 in *Crime in Society*, ed. Leonard D. Savitz and Norman Johnston. New York: Wiley.

van Dijk, Jan J. M., Pat Mayhew, and Martin Killias. 1991. *Experiences of Crime Across the World: Key Findings of the 1989 International Survey of Crime.* Deventer, The Netherlands: Kluwer.

Vanderkolk, Barbara Schwarz, and Ardis Armstrong Young. 1991. *The Work and Family Revolution: How Companies Can Keep Employees Happy and Business Profitable.* New York: Facts on File.

Vaughn, Diane. 1983. *Controlling Unlawful Organizational Behavior: Social Structure and Corporate Misconduct.* Chicago: University of Chicago Press.

Vold, George B., and Thomas J. Bernard. 1986. *Theoretical Criminology.* 3d ed. New York: Oxford University Press.

Waldman, Steven, and Karen Springen. 1992. "Too Old, Too Fast?" *Newsweek*, November 16, pp. 80–88.

Walker, Samuel. 1989. *Sense and Nonsense About Crime: A Policy Guide.* 2d ed. Pacific Grove, CA: Brooks/Cole.

Walters, Glenn D. 1992. "A Meta-Analysis of the Gene-Crime Relationship." *Criminology* 30: 595–613.

Wicker, Tom. 1991. *One of Us: Richard Nixon and the American Dream.* New York: Random House.

Wilkerson, Isabel. 1992. "27 Years Later, the Young Clearly Hear Malcolm X." *New York Times*, November 18, pp. A1, B7.

Will, George. 1992. "Democrats Can Win If They Remember What Reagan Said." *Albany Times Union*, July 12, p. E-5.

Wilson, James Q. 1975. *Thinking About Crime.* New York: Basic Books.

Wilson, James Q., and Richard J. Herrnstein. 1985. *Crime and Human Nature.* New York: Simon & Schuster.

Wilson, William Julius. 1987. *The Truly Disadvantaged: The Inner City, the Underclass, and Public Policy.* Chicago: University of Chicago Press.

Wolfe, Alan. 1989. *Whose Keeper? Social Science and Moral Obligation.* Berkeley: University of California Press.

Wolff, Edward N. 1995. "How the Pie is Sliced: America's Growing Concentration of Wealth." *The American Prospect* (Summer):58–64.

Wolfgang, Marvin E., and Franco Ferracuti. 1967. *The Subculture of Violence*. London: Tavistock.

Wolfgang, Marvin E., Robert M. Figlio, Paul E. Tracy, and Simon I. Singer. 1985. *The National Survey of Crime Severity*. Washington, D.C.: U.S. Government Printing Office.

World Health Organization. 1994. *World Health Statistics Annual*. Geneva: World Health Organization.

———. 1995. *World Health Statistics Annual*. Geneva: World Health Organization.

Wright, Charles, and R. E. Hilbert. 1980. "Value Implications of the Functional Theory of Deviance." *Social Problems* 28: 205–219.

Zahn, Margaret A. 1989. "Homicide in the Twentieth Century: Trends, Types, and Causes." pp. 216–234 in *Violence in America*, vol. 1: *The History of Crime*, ed. Ted R. Gurr. Newbury Park, CA: Sage.

Index